Write Short Stories – And Get Them Published

Zoë Fairbairns

Hodder Education

338 Euston Road, London NW1 3BH

Hodder Education is an Hachette UK company

First published in UK 2011 by Hodder Education

This edition published 2011

Typeset by Cenveo Publisher Services

Printed in Great Britain by CPI Cox & Wyman, Reading.

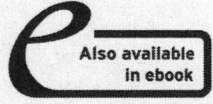

Acknowledgements

The author and Hodder Education would like to thank the following authors and/or publishers for their kind permission to reproduce the following materials:

'Your Toe-Nail' © Victoria Rose Poolman 2011, first published in *Hearing Voices*, vol. 2, edited by Sue Mackrell and David McCormack (Crystal Clear Creators (CCC)).

'Meek & Mild' © Zoë Fairbairns 2004, first published in Zoë Fairbairns, *How Do You Pronounce Nulliparous?* (Nottingham, UK: Five Leaves Publications).

'The Butterfly Slippers' © Rebecca Smith 2005, first published in *The Mountains of Mars and Other Stories*, edited by Clem Cairns (Durrus, Ireland: Fish Publishing).

'Let Me Tell a Story Now...' © Bessie Smith 2007, published in Bessie Head, *A Woman Alone – Autobiographical Writings* (London: Heinemann).

Contents

Introduction

Welcome to *Write Short Stories – And Get Them Published*

Before you start writing short stories and getting them published, there are two important things you have to know:

1 short stories are short...
2 and they are stories.

If that strikes you as a dazzling glimpse of the obvious, stick around for the next 190 or so pages and see if you still think the same.

'Short' can mean anything from six words to around 10,000. 'Story' means that something has to happen.

Not too much, though. 'The novel tends to tell us everything,' wrote V.S. Pritchett in his introduction to *The Oxford Book of Short Stories*, 'whereas the short story tells us only one thing, and that, intensely.' It is that quality of intensity, that focus on one thing, which makes a finely crafted short story such a joy to read – and such a challenge to write. How can we tell a tale which satisfies, even when it seems to be over almost as soon as it has begun? How can we find the 'one thing' which, paradoxically, seems to tell so much more?

Don't make the mistake of thinking that writing short stories is merely a limbering-up exercise for the real business of the prose writer, which is writing novels. The short story is just as real – a form in its own right, it has its own demands, traditions, markets and rewards. It dates back to the early days of oral storytelling, and now in the twenty-first century it is all over the Internet. Short stories are published in books and magazines and on websites, broadcast on the radio, adapted into films, performed in pubs and available on CDs and as podcasts. They may earn their authors prizes of up to £30,000 – or they may simply be shared among friends. They are written by established professional writers, by newcomers and by those in between.

Use this book however you like – read it from cover to cover, or dip in and out. Do the exercises in order, or start with your favourites.

But don't neglect the ones that you don't like the look of. They may be the ones that will teach you the most.

Only got a minute?

If you've only got a minute, and your ambition is to write short stories and get them published, you have no time to lose. Write one now. (Getting it published will take a little longer.)

Don't say 'I don't know how.' You do. Unless you are an unusually dull conversationalist – which I am sure that you are not – you already know how to present a brief account of something that happened, something small but significant, in a way that will interest, entertain, or at least hold the attention of others.

Use that skill when writing short stories. Write as you speak. Imagine that you have just met a friend in the street – someone you like, but haven't seen for a while. They will probably make general enquiries about your welfare and activities – 'How are you?' 'What have you been up to?' 'What's going on?' – or perhaps ask something more specific – 'What happened about your job / your operation / your dispute with your bank / that peculiar bloke who lived in your flat?'

These are all invitations to tell short stories. So write one. Write it in your own voice, as you would tell it to a friend.

How short can a short story be? As short as you like. But don't make the mistake of thinking that because a short story is short, it can be created without time and effort. Remember the old saying about letter-writing (variously attributed to George Bernard Shaw, Mark Twain and Voltaire): 'Sorry this letter is so long; I didn't have time to write a short one.' The same paradox applies to stories.

Learn how to spot a short story, or the beginnings of one, in your imagination, your memory, in a conversation, in a dream, in the world around you. It may be a moment of intensity, or a person in a state of difficulty or desire. The story arises from their attempt to explore the intensity, resolve the difficulty, satisfy the desire. It ends when they succeed or fail – or when they discover that the difficulty or the desire is not what they thought it was.

Stay focused on the small, the individual, the limited. If you try to write about everything, there is a danger that you will end up writing about nothing. But a tight little story, intensely focused on a single episode, can cast revealing lights and haunting shadows on the wider world.

Set aside regular amounts of time for writing. Have a routine and stick to it. Don't wait for inspiration. When it comes, it comes unbidden, and most of the time it doesn't come at all. Writing is a job. Treat it as one.

Read short stories – old ones and new ones, the ones you love and the ones that exasperate you. Read as a writer. Ask yourself: what can I learn from the way this writer has written this story? What can I make my own, what should I avoid?

When you are ready to approach publishers with your stories, do so in a professional way. If they say no, accept this for what it is: a commercial decision by them which has, on this occasion, gone against you. Allow yourself your moments of disappointment, then try again.

1

Where do I begin?

In this chapter, you will learn:
- *how to disregard your own excuses for not writing*
- *how to begin a story*
- *the advantages of writing in the first person*
- *the advantages of writing in the past tense*
- *how to end a story.*

'Where do I begin?' you are probably wondering.

You begin right here, by writing a short story.

Did you gasp at that? Shudder with alarm? Were you not expecting to start writing so soon?

Perhaps you have other things you need to be doing – a floor to sweep, or clothes to take to the cleaner's. Weren't you supposed to be polishing the soup spoons today, filling in your tax return, changing the batteries in your toothbrush, painting the bathroom, defragmenting your hard disk or phoning the builder? Have you taken the dog for a walk, cleaned the car, repotted the geraniums, picked plums or blackberries and made them into jam?

Insight

It's amazing how domesticated some of us become, when the alternative is writing.

Writing is a strange business – people long to do it, get hold of books on how to do it, complain about 'not having time' to do it – and then when they do have time, they start remembering all the other things they have to do first.

The reason for this is partly fear: fear that we won't be good enough. Fear that we may turn out to have nothing to say. Or too much – what if I am not a writer at all, but a sufferer from logorrhoea (excessive flow of frequently meaningless words)?

Perhaps it is the very ordinariness of writing that inhibits you. At its most basic, it is a skill that most of us have – indeed, any adult who doesn't have it is, quite rightly, recognized as being disadvantaged. Anyone can write, anywhere – what's so special about you, you may be wondering, that you should start thinking of yourself as creative, that you should grab this time and space to start making up short stories and writing them down, in the hope that one day they will be published?

The answer is in the question: what's so special about you is that you have decided to do it. That makes you special – special enough to set your own priorities. We all have the same number of hours in our day, though not, of course, the same number of days in our lives. When you finally come to the end of yours, what do you want people to say about you: 'What a wonderful person he was – his soup spoons sparkled'? 'Hers was the best-exercised dog in the neighbourhood'?

Or 'He/she wrote some brilliant short stories – and got them published'?

When are you going to write those stories, if not now? You must have some time, or you wouldn't have got this far with the opening pages of this book. In a moment I am going to ask you to stop reading and start writing.

Insight

Some of your friends, on hearing that you won't be coming out this evening because you are writing a short story, may try to dissuade you. They may be secretly envious of your single-mindedness. Other friends will be pleased that you are doing something that is important to you, even though it does not, at the moment, include them. You don't need me to tell you which of these friends are real friends, and worth hanging on to.

Clear some space in your life. Cancel other engagements. If anyone is making demands on you, tell them you are not available.

Go into a room and lock the door. Alternatively, head for the nearest café, library, pub, or park bench – anywhere where you can be comfortable and free from interruptions. Take with you a pen and paper, or whatever piece of electronic writing kit you are at ease with.

Aim to finish this first story at a single sitting. Don't worry if your language doesn't seem literary enough, formal enough. It's fine to write the story as you might tell it to a friend: if your language is good enough for him or her, it's good enough to go on the page.

Yesterday I got a phone call from a market research organization. Would I mind taking part in a customer satisfaction survey about my bank?

Mind?, I thought. Mind? I've spent half my life trying to get through to my bank to ask them what's happened to my cash ISA. I've spent a quarter of my life on hold, listening to a silly tune. My bank won't talk to me, but they're employing someone – paying someone – to ring me up and ask me what I think of them.

'Just a few questions,' the market research woman coaxed.

'Bring em on,' I replied.

'Well, it won't be me personally,' she said.

'You mean you're going to put me through to the manager? At last.'

'It's an automated survey,' she explained. 'You answer it on your telephone keypad.'

'The story of my lost ISA would be wasted on a telephone keypad. Let me tell you. Five months ago...'

'Thanks for taking part in our survey,' the woman interrupted. And the next thing I knew I was listening to a recording which wanted to know whether I was extremely satisfied, quite satisfied, neither satisfied nor dissatisfied, a bit dissatisfied or extremely dissatisfied with the layout of the furniture in the public areas of my local branch. I hung up.

It's not finely tuned or highly polished or earth-shattering. It won't win a prize or bring about a reform of the Financial Services Act, and it certainly won't locate the narrator's cash ISA. It's just a quickly written account of something that happened yesterday, a tale which allows the author to let off some steam at the same time as drawing your attention to the fact that short stories are all around you, each of them with a beginning (the phone call), a middle (the conversation), some backstory (the lost ISA) and an end (the narrator hangs up).

Here's another example:

Yesterday I saw him in the street. At first I didn't recognize him, probably because he was fully clothed. Normally when I see him, he is stark naked except for his underpants.

I glimpse him through the window of his ground-floor flat when I walk past on my way home from my evening class. I don't deliberately stare, but it's hard not to look when his kitchen is all lit up and there he is, an old, bald, semi-naked guy, cooking with a frying pan at ten o'clock at night.

He cooks egg, bacon, sausages, fried bread, the works. He's quite seriously overweight, which is hardly surprising if that is his idea of a late-night snack. His belly bulges over his Y-fronts, dangerously exposed to the spitting fat. I feel sorry for him.

At least, I used to. Until yesterday, when I saw him in the street, holding hands with a woman. I won't say she was a beautiful woman; she was quite ordinary really, about his age, scruffy like him, and with grey hair. But you could see from the way they held hands that they were totally wrapped up in each other.

He glanced at me as if he thought he might recognize me but he was not sure where from. And then he turned away as if he didn't really care – he was much more interested in his companion than a random stranger walking by. And it dawned on me that maybe his midnight cook-ups weren't comfort food at all; the only comfort he needed, he was getting from her. The food was a post-sex snack. And the look he had given me was indeed one of recognition, recognition of the woman who walks past his window late at night, always on her own, while he is warm and snug inside, preparing love-food for himself and his darling, to replenish their energy before they get back to whatever they had been doing, while I hurry home alone through the darkness.

Now it's your turn. Begin with the words 'Yesterday I …', and off you go.

When the narrator of your story has dealt with his or her dilemma, conflict, desire or predicament, and resolved it – or when they have realized that it cannot be resolved – stop writing, and pat yourself on the back. You have written a short story. Well done.

And before you dismiss me as an insincere flatterer – I can't see what you have written, so how can I have a valid opinion on whether it is well done or not? – let's have a look at what writing that story has taught you:

1 **The only way to write is to write.** To put it another way – and at the risk of sounding like an ad for trainers – just do it.

2 **Use the first person.** Not all stories have to be narrated by 'I' – we'll be exploring alternatives elsewhere in this book. But writing as 'I' (whether or not that 'I' is really you, and whether or not the story is true) comes naturally to most of us, echoing the way we speak.

If you write as 'I' you won't be tempted to go wandering off into other people's minds: you know that you can't know what someone else is thinking. You also know that you can't give first-hand descriptions of events at which you were not present, so you won't be tempted to try that either. Using 'I' means keeping things nice and simple, which is what you need if you are a beginner riddled with uncertainty and looking for the slightest excuse to get back to polishing those soup spoons.

3 **Use the past tense.** Again, it's not the only way, but it's a good way to start. By beginning your story with the word 'yesterday', you commit yourself to describing events that have already happened, rather than those which are happening now. This makes for simplicity. Simplicity is not the same as ease, but it should add to your confidence that you can write short stories.

4 **How to end a story.** Some new writers fear that once they start writing, they won't be able to stop. What if you can't find an ending to your story? What if it goes on and on and on? What if it turns into a novel?

A short story turning into a novel isn't the end of the world, but if you don't want that to happen to your story, stay focused on one person in one situation of difficulty or uncertainty. Let that person work to resolve that difficulty or uncertainty, or else discover that it isn't going to be resolved. At the end of my first example, both characters are frustrated – the market researcher hasn't got her answers, and the narrator is no closer to tracking down her ISA. But it's the end of the conversation, and therefore of the story. At the end of my second example, the narrator realizes that the pity she feels for the man might more appropriately be directed towards herself.

Now that you have written your story, what should you do with it?

You could:

▶ show it to someone
▶ delete it (not recommended – even if you hate it, it almost certainly contains something that you can reuse)
▶ enter it for a competition
▶ post it on your website or blog
▶ put it to one side and come back to it later
▶ write another one (recommended). It could be about something else that you did yesterday, or it could be something you didn't do yesterday, written as if you did.

> ▶ Yesterday I killed a man.
> ▶ Yesterday I killed a goldfish.
> ▶ Yesterday I ate a pound of onions.
> ▶ Yesterday I locked myself out of my flat.
> ▶ Yesterday I realized that I love you.
> ▶ Yesterday I went to a meeting of an assisted suicide group.
> ▶ Yesterday I had a visit from the bailiffs.
> ▶ Yesterday I bought a pregnancy testing kit.
> ▶ Yesterday I woke up to the smell of a fox.
> ▶ Yesterday I led a convoy through the mountains.
> ▶ Yesterday I sacked my best friend.

If any of those happens to be true for you, leave it out. Choose another one, and write the story as if it were true.

Alternatively, if you think you've done enough short story writing for one day, it's fine to go off and join your friends in the pub. Or give those soup spoons a polishing they will never forget.

10 THINGS TO KEEP IN MIND

1 Short stories are short.

2 And they are stories. Something has to happen.

3 When it has happened, end the story.

4 If you are a beginner, restrict yourself to the first person and the past tense until you are more confident.

5 Let the narrator tell the story as if they were talking to a friend.

6 Centre your story around one person in a situation of difficulty, and show how that difficulty is resolved or not resolved.

7 If your factual story seems to want to turn into fiction, let it.

8 And vice versa.

9 But don't give in to pressure to say which is which.

10 Value friends who respect your writing.

2

What you need

In this chapter, you will learn:
- *why writers need assignments*
- *how to claim time and space for writing*
- *how to find an audience for your work*
- *how to use your notebook.*

Back in the bad old days, when men were men and women put up with it, I once sat through a talk by a male writer who said that if you wanted to write, what you needed most of all was a wife.

Uninhibited by the fact that more than half his audience were female and therefore more likely to be wives than to have them, he warmed to his theme, which was the desirability of keeping someone at home who would be a skivvy, a secretary, a cook, an editor, a stimulus-provider, a publicist, a host, a minder, a childminder, an accountant, a cleaner, an indexer, a shoulder to cry on, and a punchbag to punch. (He meant this last one metaphorically. At least, I hope he did.) If the wife could be a breadwinner too, so much the better.

And wouldn't we all like to have those services available to us when we are trying to devote ourselves single-mindedly to our writing? Wouldn't it be nice of us to offer those services to our loved ones? But not all the time, and not one-sidedly. This chapter looks at what writers need, and how we can meet those needs for ourselves, preferably without making unreasonable demands on others.

> **Insight**
> Being a writer doesn't mean you have a right to be impossible to live with – or at least, any more right than anybody else.

So what *do* writers need?

WRITERS NEED TO WRITE

You probably know this already.

Writing makes you happy – or, if that is too strong a word, at least it gives you satisfaction. On the days when you don't write, you don't feel good. You feel as if you have wasted time, failed to justify your existence. You don't feel mentally fit, you don't feel like yourself.

That's one of the reasons why I began this book with a writing exercise: I knew you would want one. I wanted to separate the real writers – i.e. people who really write – from people who only talk about it and make excuses. I knew that the real short story writers would want to write a short story as soon as possible, and would appreciate an assignment.

WRITERS NEED ASSIGNMENTS

Some writers get up every day knowing exactly what they want to write, and how to write it. They probably aren't the ones reading this book.

The rest of us need assignments. And I don't just mean the sort of assignment that comes from an editor with a promise of publication and a fee, helpful though those can be in concentrating the mind. I'm talking about any writing task that has been set by someone else.

The fact that it has been set by someone else doesn't make it restrictive: paradoxically, it can be very freeing. By eliminating alternatives, it eliminates distractions. Having a task concentrates the mind, and makes writers feel useful and connected. It helps get us started on those occasions when we sit down at the desk wanting and needing to write something, but not sure what.

Insight

Fiction, being imaginary, is infinite in its scope. Infinity is all very well, but it is sometimes a bit too big to work with. An assignment cuts it down to size.

You are reading this book because you want to write short stories and get them published, and you will find short story ideas throughout, as you will find them in other books listed at the back.

You will also find them in writing magazines such as *Writers' Forum* and *MsLexia*, where they may be themes for competitions. The closing dates for the competitions will probably have come and gone by the time you read this, but you can still draw inspiration from the ideas.

Think of them as assignments. Give yourself a deadline and stick to it – even if there is no editor out there waiting eagerly for you to deliver your work. Yet.

WRITERS NEED SPACE AND TIME

Virginia Woolf famously declared that 'a woman must have money and a room of her own if she is to write fiction.' To which later generations of writers of all genders can only respond with a heartfelt sigh of 'I wish...'

If you live alone, or have unused rooms, then space and solitude will not be a problem. If your home is full but you have a friend with spare rooms, you might be able to rent or borrow one.

Small shops sometimes have empty rooms behind them or upstairs. The owners may have long-term plans for the rooms and so be reluctant to rent them out as living space; but if you explain that you are not planning to take up residence, only to set down your computer and books and spend a few hours a day writing, and if you sign whatever undertakings the owners require about being willing to move out at short notice, a deal may be struck.

If none of these is a possibility, you are either going to have to make do with cafés, pubs and libraries, or negotiate with your family or flatmates. Can everyone agree to keep out of a particular room for a set number of hours? Can the garden shed or garage be converted? Can that sofa be your writing sofa? Does anyone mind if you have rather a long bath?

Insight

A student was living in a studio flat with her boyfriend, also an aspiring writer. There was room only for one desk, so they agreed on a shift system. While one of them was at the desk, the other lay very still on the bed, listening to music over headphones. At an agreed time, they swapped over. The last I heard, they were still together and still writing.

The room of your own is as much symbolic as real. It is about mental space as well as physical space. It is about not answering the phone or the door; it is about asking people not to distract you. It might be about disconnecting your writing computer from the Internet (but see below), and disabling the solitaire game.

It is also about comfort. Don't feel you have to suffer for your art. If you've got a special chair, sit on it. If you've got a favourite picture, stick it on the wall. If you're cold, turn the heating up, fill a hot-water bottle or put a blanket over your knees. If music helps, play it. Try not to smoke or drink yourself to death, or OD on the chocolate digestives – but, within reason, allow yourself the treats and comforts that help get you to your workplace and keep you there.

WRITERS NEED THE INTERNET

I say this in full awareness of the number of crimes against writing of which the Internet stands accused. It is responsible, we have been told, for:

- ▶ the near-disappearance of proper grammar and correct spelling
- ▶ the decline of independent bookselling
- ▶ the narrowing of writers' horizons and social lives (because we no longer need to leave our homes to do research, it is argued that we miss out on all the adventures we might have enjoyed en route to the library)
- ▶ the disappearance of markets for our writing, as people who might once have been our readers, discover, via social networking sites, that they would rather spend their leisure time exchanging messages with their friends than reading stories made up by strangers
- ▶ making self-publishing too easy, thus removing the incentive to produce work of the sort of quality that will induce someone else to invest in it
- ▶ the reluctance of people who can help themselves to good fiction for free online, to pay for it and so contribute to writers' livelihoods.

There is truth in all of these allegations, but they don't add up to a case against writers having Internet access when we need it. And we do need it, at least for:

- ▶ **basic research** – though we may still need to visit specialist libraries, or pretend we do, if we are hoping to enjoy a brief encounter on the way.
- ▶ **email** – many publishers, magazines and competitions will only accept writers' work by this means
- ▶ **marketing** – even if your ultimate aim is to publish your stories in print media, short story websites such as www.writingforums.com provide opportunities for you to bring your work to an audience – perhaps catching the eye of editors and agents – in the meantime. The same applies if you choose to showcase your stories on your own website or blog
- ▶ **news** – writers' organizations offer tips about events, opportunities and writing itself. They come and go, so it is impossible to provide a complete, up-to-date list; but you could start with www.writewords.org.uk, which will give you up-to-date information about others. Likewise writers' blogs and social networking. Google the names of your favourite living short story writers, and see what is available
- ▶ **reading and learning** – many of the stories and articles recommended in this book are available online – or at least they were at the time of writing this. No guarantee can be offered that they will still be there by the time you read these words, but even if they have been removed, others will have taken their place.

Insight

If the Internet is more of a distraction than a benefit, don't have it in your home. But don't exclude it from your life. Use your local library or Internet café.

WRITERS NEED TIME FOR WRITING

When you are a serious writer – and by 'serious' I mean committed to it, even if you are not yet published – one of the banes of your life is people who say, 'I could write, but I never have time.'

What they mean is, they want the fun bits of being a writer (seeing their stories in print, sipping wine at launch parties, Googling themselves and finding yet another adulatory review) but they don't want to put in the hours and do the work that might make those things happen. They don't want to face the fact that finding the time is part of the job.

How do you find the time to write?

Make a list of the things you do find time for, and consider ways to cut down.

Sleeping. How many hours per night do you sleep? Could you manage on less? Try getting up earlier to write. Or stay up and write when everyone else in your home has gone to bed. Everyone's rhythms of sleepiness, alertness and creativity are different, so try different schedules to find what works best for you.

Earning your living. You probably have to do this, but can you do less of it? If your job consumes too much of your time, can you cut back your hours? Do less overtime? Or change to another job, one which makes fewer demands? Any of these choices may involve a drop in income. Only you can decide what financial sacrifices you are willing and able to make, and expect your dependants to make, in order that you will have time to write. Beware of giving up employment altogether, even if you are financially able to do so: your job keeps you in touch with the day-to-day lives and adventures of your fellow humans in a way that you might miss if you lost it. There's no point in being a full-time writer if you have nothing to write about.

Looking after your home – housework, DIY, etc. On this I can only quote the wise words of Quentin Crisp: 'There is no need to do any housework at all. After the first four years the dirt doesn't get any worse.'

Looking after people. It depends who you are looking after. You have to keep yourself fed, watered, as well-groomed as your lifestyle and social circumstances require, and in as good a state of health as you can manage. You have to do the same for people who are your responsibility and who can't do it for themselves. But what about people in your household who are perfectly capable of looking after themselves? I'm not naming any names here, but why are you wasting valuable writing time running round after them – unless it's part of a deal in which, on alternate days, they run round after you?

Hobbies, sports, cultural, religious and political activities, socializing. Can you cut down on these? You don't have to give them up entirely – indeed it's probably better not to, because, like employment, they give you ideas and stimulation, they are part of who you are, they are the place where you are writing from. But, if you are going to meetings once a week, consider cutting back to once a month. If you are getting together with friends every Friday, change that to every other Friday. If you really don't feel you can cut back, fine; what you're saying is that, for you, writing is not important enough to prioritize over these other activities. It's good to be honest with yourself about this. There's no law that says you have to be a writer, and you will probably be happier if you concentrate on things that are more important to you.

WRITERS NEED A ROUTINE

Having identified a block of time that you can use for writing, claim it. Make a realistic commitment to it, and write that commitment down.

Make it specific: not just 'I will sleep less and write more', but 'I will get up at 6 a.m. rather than 7 a.m. on Mondays, Tuesdays, Fridays and Saturdays, and use those extra four hours per week for writing.' Not just 'I will do less gardening' but 'I will leave the garden to its own devices on Sunday afternoons and grow some short stories instead.'

Having made the commitment, stick to it, *whether you feel like it or not.*

Insight

If you wait for inspiration, you will wait for ever.

WRITERS NEED TIME FOR NOT WRITING

There is more to writing than writing. You need thinking time, researching time and dreaming time.

Writers need lives: we need to live our own, and interact with the lives of others. Don't get so wrapped up in your writing that you forget to have friendships and love affairs, good causes to support and bad ones to oppose, conversations over the fence with the neighbours, disputes, hobbies, obligations and fun.

WRITERS NEED AN AUDIENCE

Approaches to publishing your stories are looked at in detail in Chapter 18. But even before you get to that stage, it will be helpful if you can show your stories to someone who will give you an honest, fair, constructive response and let you know whether the story they read is the one that you set out to write.

How can you find this paragon? Should you show your freshly written, unpublished stories to your partner, spouse, family or friends?

Perhaps, but treat their response with caution. They know you in ways that a stranger doesn't, and may be unable to avoid bringing that knowledge to their appreciation of your work. They may be reluctant to hurt your feelings. Or they may be subconsciously eager to do exactly that, in revenge for a time when you hurt theirs. They may know – or think they know – about the real events that inspired your fiction, and this too may influence their judgement.

So look for opportunities to show your work to strangers or near-strangers, people who will come to your stories without a backstory of their own. Enrol in a writing course, join a writers' group, or set up one of your own. To find courses near you, enquire at your nearest university or adult education centre, or write 'creative writing classes' and the area where you live into your search engine. To find groups, contact the National Association of Writers' Groups, NAWG, PO Box 3266, Stoke-on-Trent ST10 9BD (www.nawg.co.uk). If you prefer online discussion of your work, have a look at www.short-story.net and www.writingforums.net. Fish Publishing, at www.fishpublishing.com, offers a paid-for critique service, online tuition and an editorial consultancy.

Do writers need specialist equipment?

Not much. You need a **pen and paper,** and/or a **computer.**

Some writers attach great importance to such matters as the size and weight of paper they use, types of pen, and colour of ink. Some computer users have strong views on which version of which word-processing software best meets their needs. If these things are important to you, spend some time investigating the alternatives and choose what suits you. But don't imagine that your chosen tools will facilitate the actual task of the short story writer, which is to choose the right words to tell the story you want to tell, to your intended readers.

You need an up-to-date **dictionary** so that you can check the spelling, meaning and usage of words about which you are unsure. And while you're at it, you might now and again check the ones about which you think you are sure. They might have changed.

A **handbook of English grammar** is useful: even if you are fairly confident in your knowledge, you probably have blank spots. *English Grammar for Dummies* by Lesley J. Ward and Geraldine Woods (John Wiley & Sons) is not only excellent and well organized for quick reference; it is also witty and fun to read.

And you need a **notebook**. As with other stationery, there's no hard-and-fast rule about what kind is best: an expensive hardback folder with a fancy design on the cover, selected with care in an art shop, is no more or less suitable than a reporter's jotter picked up in a pack of five at the Everything For A £ store. It should be small enough to carry with you at all times, so that you can record stray thoughts, half-formed stories, overheard conversations, dreams, lists and the things you wish you'd said.

What else does a writer need?

A writer needs realism, cynicism, idealism, imagination and awe. She or he needs to be naive and sophisticated, observant, obsessive, focused and a dreamer – sometimes at different times, sometimes all at once. A writer needs to be able to work hard, but also to stand and stare. A writer needs a capacity for disappointment, and the ability, if necessary (and it may be necessary), to live on very little money. A writer needs commitment, and emotional and intellectual courage. Some writers require physical courage, too: the words you write may enrage some people, or even some governments, and so put you into danger.

Many of these needs are common to all writers – indeed, all people. What are the special needs of writers of short stories?

What do short story writers need?

You need a special capacity to be intrigued and creatively inspired by small things, brief events, fleeting moments. One of the most brilliantly haunting English-language short stories to have emerged from the US/Vietnam War of the 1960s/70s, 'The Things They Carried' by Tim O'Brien (in his collection *The Things They Carried* (Flamingo)) focuses on a collection of objects small enough to be carried by a soldier on a long patrol. As a short story writer, you need to be able to find stories in the things you carry.

You need plots and structures for your stories, to keep them as tight and controlled and vivid as the story's length and subject matter require. Some of these structures will be explored in this book. Some can be identified in the work of other writers; the new writer can learn from these, or improvise around them.

As a writer of short stories, you need to be a person who reads short stories with enthusiasm and critical enjoyment, always alert to their pleasures and possibilities. You should be familiar with the classics, and constantly on the lookout for new stories, in books, in magazines, on the radio and online.

And you need a little black dress.

10 THINGS TO KEEP IN MIND

1 Use assignments and writing tasks set by other people. They will often stimulate those aspects of your creativity that your own ideas never reach.

2 If you've got a room of your own for writing, good for you. If you have to make do with a smaller, more public space, you can still make it yours. Think of it as your own even on those annoying occasions when someone else is sitting there.

3 Be comfortable when you write.

4 Decide how important writing is to you, compared with the other things you do. Claim time from the less important things, and use it for writing.

5 Have a writing routine and stick to it.

6 Don't trust your memory to hold on to unusual sights, overheard snippets, half-formed stories. Keep a notebook with you at all times, and use it.

7 You don't need a lot of fancy equipment to write short stories. Pen, paper and/or a computer are enough for most situations.

8 Make sure you have access to the Internet, but don't let it distract you.

9 When you are writing, always have within reach a dictionary, and a guide to grammar and punctuation.

10 Read lots of short stories.

3

The little black dress

In this chapter, you will learn:
- *a basic short story structure, suitable for many occasions.*

- Somebody wants something.
- There is an obstacle to the fulfilment of their desire.
- They seek to overcome the obstacle, but fail.
- They try again.
- Something unexpected happens, which may or may not help.
- They get what they want, or they don't.

That's a structure for a short story. It can be expressed even more briefly, reduced to just two components:

1 **Predicament** (i.e. a situation of difficulty, desire, uncertainty, embarrassment or danger)
2 **Resolution** (i.e. the way things turn out).

Long-established, tried-and-tested, reliable, and universal in its appeal, this is the little black dress of short story writing.

What has a little black dress got to do with writing short stories?

The little black dress, in literal terms, is an essential item in the clothes-conscious woman's wardrobe. It's simple, and it suits her, whatever her age, shape or background. She can dress it up or dress it down, accessorize or keep it plain. It is neither fashionable nor unfashionable – it is a classic.

This type of short story shares some of these attributes.

(This is an equal opportunities book, and I have been asking around to find out whether there is a male equivalent of the little black dress. Suggestions I have received include a plain white shirt, a crew cut and a well-polished pair of good leather shoes.)

No one wants to wear a little black dress – or a plain white shirt – all day every day, and no one wants to write the same short story over and over again. But it's nice to have something to fall back on, on those occasions when you need to write a short story – perhaps someone has set you an assignment, or there's a themed competition that you want to go in for, or perhaps you've just got something on your mind – and you don't know where to begin.

Nobody will notice this story structure particularly, or call it cutting-edge or ahead of its time, avant-garde or experimental; but they won't object to it either. If they do, it will only be on the grounds that it is old-fashioned. And it is true that it goes back a long way.

Insight

A student once told me that she didn't want to work with the predicament/resolution structure because it was 'formulaic' and 'too easy'. Virginia Woolf wouldn't have written a story in this way, and neither would Chekhov. Therefore the student didn't want to either.

But the student was not Virginia Woolf or Chekhov, and neither are you and neither am I. We're not trying to prove our literary credentials. We're looking for ways to write short stories, and this is one that works.

The little black dress: early examples

In the sixth century BC, the slave Aesop in ancient Greece was probably not thinking about little black dresses when he created his fable about the fox and the cheese. But we can identify the key elements:

- ▶ A fox is hungry for a piece of cheese. (*Desire.*)
- ▶ The cheese is currently in the beak of a raven who is perched on the branch of a tree, safely out of reach of the fox. (*Obstacle.*)
- ▶ The fox tries to persuade the raven to share the cheese, but the raven refuses. (*Unsuccessful attempts to overcome obstacle.*)

▶ Trying a different tack, the fox praises the raven for its singing voice, and begs for a song. Succumbing to flattery, the raven opens its mouth to sing, allowing the cheese to fall to the ground. (*Unexpected development solves the problem.*)

▶ The fox eats the cheese. (*The matter is resolved: the fox gets what he wants.*)

Six centuries later, Jesus Christ told the story of the Good Samaritan:

▶ A man gets beaten up, robbed and left by the roadside, hoping for rescue. (*Danger and desire.*)

▶ Two people pass by, ignoring him. (*Obstacle.*)

▶ A third person, a Samaritan and an outsider, takes pity on him. (*Unexpected development.*)

▶ The Samaritan binds up the victim's wounds and takes him to an inn, where he pays for him to stay and recover. (*The matter is resolved: the victim of the attack gets what he wants, i.e. rescue.*)

Moving forward a few more centuries, the *1001 Nights* stories, a collection of Middle Eastern and South Asian stories thought to have been first written down in the tenth century, have at their heart the desire of a Persian king to murder a succession of new wives. One of the wives, seeking to avoid this fate, sets out to distract the king with stories. Thus the stories themselves (many of which centre around people having adventures – another way of saying 'getting into predicaments and either succumbing or escaping') are part of the main story's resolution, which is that the wife is spared.

From fourteenth-century England, Geoffrey Chaucer's *Canterbury Tales* – also a collection of stories contained within the main story of the desire of a group pilgrims to get to Canterbury – includes 'The Knight's Tale', in which two young men find themselves imprisoned in a foreign land. Looking out of the window, they spot a beautiful woman and fall in love with her. Their rivalry and their confinement are just two of the many obstacles in the way of love's fulfilment.

From the nineteenth century, Arthur Conan Doyle's Sherlock Holmes stories, being detective stories, are always about an individual with a mystery to solve, and the overcoming (or not) of obstacles in the path to that solution.

In the 1960s and 70s, aspiring writers of romantic fiction were often advised by editors to stick closely to the formula which goes 'boy meets girl, boy loses girl, boy gets girl back and they live happily ever after'. Coming closer to our own times, Maeve Binchy's 'Queensway', in her collection *Victoria Line, Central Line* (Arrow Books), tells the story of a bank worker new to the big city, looking for somewhere to live. She seeks advice, asks around and, after several false starts, seems finally to have found the perfect flatshare. (Only it isn't, of course: the resolution is a false one.) More recently and more grimly, the Zimbabwean writer Petina Gappah, in 'Something Nice from London' (in her collection *An Elegy for Easterly* (Faber)), recounts the plight of a family who turn up again and again at a barely functioning Third World airport to collect the body of a dead relative, which is supposedly being flown home for burial, but which never seems to arrive.

Using this structure should not be the beginning and end of your ambitions as a short story writer, but, as has been shown, it has a long and honourable pedigree, can be used in different ways, and is a good place to start.

Resolving a predicament is not necessarily the same as solving a problem. A quest which descends into failure or debacle can make a story that is just as satisfying as one with a happy ending.

The ending may not be a simple matter of a character getting what they wanted, or failing to do so. They may find that, far more important than the thing they were looking for, was the quest itself.

Keep in mind the saying: 'Be careful what you wish for, for you may get it.' It can be used to give a bitter twist to the resolution of your characters' predicaments. Penny Vincenzi, in her short story 'The Glimpses' (in the collection *New Woman, New Fiction*, edited by Suzanne Askham (Pan Macmillan)) tells of a young husband and father who, feeling smothered by suburban domesticity, seeks sexual adventure with a free-spirited woman. Escaping at last from the cloying cosiness of his wife, he finds that his new love has become pregnant by him: so now, instead of one little family to feel trapped by, he has two.

Another way to dress up your little black dress

The French filmmaker Jean-Luc Godard has said that films should have a beginning, a middle and an end – 'but not necessarily in that order.'

The same is true of short stories.

Here's the outline of a little-black-dress type of story:

- My cat went missing.
- I phoned my ex to ask if he (or she) had seen my cat.
- My ex told me that my cat was with him.
- I pleaded with him to return my cat, and he agreed.
- A box arrived on my doorstep.
- I opened the box and found my cat's dead body.

You could write that story in exactly that way, a simple linear narrative that begins with No. 1 (the loss of the cat) and ends with No. 6 (the resolution of the mystery – the discovery of its fate). Or you could begin at No. 2, or anywhere else.

Beginning a story in the middle, or even at the end, is often a good strategy, but it should be done for a reason. For example, you may feel that the liveliest beginning for this story would be not the disappearance of the cat, but the phone call which establishes that the cat has gone. You could have fun – and make your reader wince – by writing one of those edgy don't-run-away-with-the-idea-that-I'm-still-in-love-with-you conversations. The more the caller talks about the cat, the more the ex imagines – rightly or wrongly – that the cat is just an excuse for the call, the real purpose of which is to re-establish contact.

Or you might feel that the most arresting moment of the story is the arrival of the box on the doorstep. If you use that as the beginning – not assuming that your readers know anything about the missing cat or the recent break-up – then it is the box on the doorstep that is the predicament. What is it? Where has it come from? Is it good news or bad? Should the narrator open the box, or get on the phone to the bomb squad? When the contents of the box are finally revealed, what follows is a combination of explanation (who has done this, and why?) and what the narrator is going to do about it. (Weep uncontrollably? Phone the RSPCA? Get revenge by doing something frightful to the ex's hamster?)

Adapt your little black dress to the occasion. That's what little black dresses are for. Raise or lower the hem or the neckline. Add jewellery, or austerely remove it. But every adaptation should have a reason. Don't begin in the middle, or at the end, solely because it makes your work look clever, or postmodern, or avant-garde.

Don't approach writing with the blood-chilling sentiment of 'not wanting to make things too easy for the reader' or 'expecting the reader to work'. Of course your reader will work – if you make it worth their while.

Insight
Don't take for granted your reader's willingness to work hard at reading your story – particularly if you have not worked hard at writing it.

As a diner in a restaurant, you wouldn't expect the chef to dump a pile of ingredients on your table for you to cook: that's the chef's job.*

---

*Since first writing those words, I have discovered that there is indeed a restaurant in London where you cook your own food. There is also an online message board where people discuss the concept. Comments include: 'Why don't you just go to your own kitchen?' and 'Are people really that weird in London?' I rest my case.

And it's the writer's job to write the story. Of course, there will be times when the story you have chosen to write will be too complex, wise and subtle to admit of a straightforward approach. There will be times when an opaque or elliptical or non-linear approach may seem to have more beauty, or be more fun. Then it's up to you to write it in a way that will make your reader persevere, not because you think they ought to, but because you have made them want to.

> **Try this**
> **Think of a story that you know well,** but are accustomed to hearing in chronological order – 'Cinderella', for example, or the tale of how your parents first met, or the life and death of Princess Diana. List the main events under the headings: (1) Desire, (2) Obstacle, (3) Attempts to Overcome Obstacle, (4) Unexpected Development, (5) Resolution. Now consider ways in which you could retell the story beginning anywhere other than (1).
> **Would doing this make the story more lively, more intriguing?** Or would it be an unnecessary complication?

More accessories for your little black dress

▶ Use the supernatural. The unexpected development which moves the story forward may involve magicians, goblins, avatars, gods and goddesses, mythical beasts, animals with human powers and vice versa. This launches your story into magical realism. For more on this, see Chapter 14.
▶ Failing to find what he was looking for, your protagonist may find something more important.
▶ Whether he finds it or not, he may realize that the quest was more important than the achievement.

Insight
Don't be in too much of a hurry to dismiss a type of short story as 'old-fashioned'. Even old-fashioned things can have usefulness, beauty, value and charm. Without them, they wouldn't have survived long enough to become old-fashioned.

10 THINGS TO KEEP IN MIND

1 If you put a character into a predicament, and write about them getting out of it, you are guaranteed a story.

2 Keep it simple.

3 Short stories need a beginning, a middle and an end – but not necessarily in that order.

4 The beginning should tell your reader enough to make them want to know more.

5 The work of writers you admire is there for you to enjoy and learn from – not to copy, or feel disempowered by.

6 If your story is complex and subtle, then it's fine to write it in complex and subtle ways. But don't resort to tricks just to make yourself look clever.

7 Don't expect your reader to work harder than you do.

8 Look for the structures in the stories you read.

9 Never forget that you are inviting your reader into your imaginary world. Make them welcome.

10 The little black dress is not for everyday wear. But isn't it nice to know you've got one?

4

....

Whose story is this?

In this chapter, you will learn:
- *what is meant by point of view*
- *why it matters*
- *how to choose the right point of view for the story you want to tell.*

Whose story is this? It is yours, of course. You are making it up, or remembering it. Even if you don't yet know everything that it will contain, how it will be arranged or what it all means, you know more than anyone else.

But that doesn't mean you are going to reveal all the information immediately. One of the satisfactions of reading a story comes from the slow release of information. It follows from this that one of the arts of story writing is knowing what to reveal and when to reveal it.

This in turn depends on the point of view from which the story is being told.

Point of view

In Chapter 1, you were advised, if you are a newcomer to short story writing, to start by writing your stories in the first person – as 'I'.

This is not because all your stories have to be about you: the 'I' can be a fictional character. Nor is the first person necessarily better than other approaches. But it has one major advantage, which is that it puts off the moment when you have to make sometimes-difficult decisions about what is known, what can be revealed, and what is the best way of revealing it.

With an I-narrator, many of these decisions have been made for you. It is the narrator's story, and everything is experienced from his or her point of view. The reader can know only what the narrator knows.

Try this
Part one
Write a few sentences to describe the space which you are now occupying. It might go something like this:

The room is about 3 metres square – big enough to contain the things I need, small enough to be cosy. It's got an antique office desk, a workstation, a filing cabinet, and a big comfortable armchair that I am currently slumped in, with my laptop on my lap. There's an ornamental fireplace with coloured-glass baubles in the grate. I inherited those from my mother. The carpet is oatmeal-coloured, and soft under my bare feet. There's a tall CD rack, with a few Pet Shop Boys CDs out of their boxes. The longest wall is lined with bookshelves.

Part two
Now describe the same room from the point of view of the person whose job it is to keep it clean:

Most of the furniture is old and wooden, difficult to move, and with plenty of places for dust to gather. The piles of books on the shelves look as if they'll topple over at the slightest touch. They often do. Half the CDs are out of their boxes and scattered across the floor. I hardly dare touch the glass baubles in the fireplace – she got them from her mother, and I wouldn't want to break them. One of these days, though, I'm going to have to take my courage in both hands and dust them. And the carpet needs shampooing.

Part three
Describe the room from the point of view of an estate agent who is hoping to sell the house:

Spacious, well-lit studio in loft conversion with views towards the park. Fitted carpet, plentiful storage space for CDs, books, etc. Feature fireplace.

All three narrators are talking about the same room, and none of them is deliberately lying. Yet each description is different. The occupant of the room takes pleasure in her space and possessions. The cleaner sees work. The estate agent identifies selling points. Each person has a different relationship with the room, and therefore describes it in a different way.

You can apply the same principle to the people, events, objects and settings in your stories.

Insight

What you see – or hear, or smell, or feel or taste – depends on who you are. What you choose to describe reflects what is important to you.

A recruitment consultant once told me that he always looks at the backs of candidates' shoes. He reasons that although most people will polish the fronts of their shoes to smarten up for an interview, only a person who is serious about good grooming pays attention to the backs of their shoes. I offer this not only as a useful piece of information for job interviewees, but also to show how observed details can say as much about the observer as they do about the person or thing being observed.

Try this

Write a short description of a pair of lovers kissing in the street, seen from the point of view of:

1 one of the lovers
2 a casual passer-by
3 the spouse of one of the lovers, who has spotted them by chance from a passing bus.

Pay particular attention to the different perceptions that arise from the different roles of the characters in the situation. The uninvolved passer-by might note with amusement that the pair are so wrapped up in each other that they don't realize that one of them has one foot in a pile of dog mess. The jealous spouse may see only the tightness and enthusiasm of the embrace, or they might perhaps spitefully note the deplorable dress sense of their rival. The lovers themselves may only have eyes for each other.

Insight

Spend some time in the public gallery of a court and note how the same event may be presented in completely different ways, depending on whether the account comes from the prosecution or the defence.

Point of view isn't just about what you perceive through your senses; it's about what you know, what impression things make on you.

If you grew up with brothers or sisters of about your own age, you have probably had the experience of clearly remembering some childhood event, treat or crisis, only to hear one of your siblings recall it in a completely different way – or perhaps even deny that it ever took place. They are probably not deliberately rewriting history, any more than you are. A more likely explanation is that you and they have retained in your and their memory different aspects of what happened, because of who you and they are and were.

If you are writing a crime story, the point of view you choose will dictate what the readers know, and perhaps whose side they are on. If it is the point of view of the detective, who doesn't know 'whodunnit' but is trying to find out, the reader can enjoy the slow unfolding of the truth. If it is told from the point of view of the bad guy, the reader may have the pleasingly uncomfortable feeling of being implicated in the crime, of knowing the awful truth, of identifying with the villain, even rooting for them as they outwit that know-nothing detective.

Either of these can be a satisfying way of writing (and reading) a mystery story. But you have to be consistent. If you give your reader some insights into the villain's mind (showing their dreams or fantasies, for example, or their ideological beliefs or their memories of childhood) but not enough to reveal what they did and how and why they did it, then when the truth comes out the reader may wonder why they weren't told before. If the sole reason is that the author wanted to keep the reader in suspense, the reader may feel manipulated or even cheated. But if the author has accepted the discipline of indicating the villain's thoughts only through his or her external behaviour, then the revelation of their guilt is more likely to have that perfect combination of surprise and inevitability.

Insight

Decide from the start whose story it is – that is, from whose point of view you are telling it – and stick with that decision. Don't wander at random from one point of view to another.

Choosing your point of view

When choosing a point of view for your story, you have five main options. Here they are in action, in the opening lines of a story in which someone is reluctantly moving house. You will also find examples of how the different points of view have been used in other writers' short stories.

1 FIRST PERSON

As I inserted the key into the lock, I was hoping it would stick. That would have allowed me to believe that it was the wrong key, the wrong lock, that I had come to the wrong house.

But the little Yale, with the estate agent's fob dangling from it, slid in smoothly and turned with ease. The door swung open. It was true, then. Of all the houses in all the world, I had bought this one.

I stepped inside. At the other end of the path, two teenage boys passed. One of them made a remark. I didn't catch it, and didn't want to – it was sure to be something obscene. I closed the door and locked it.

Advantages of first person

- ▶ It's authentic and natural. It echoes everyday speech.
- ▶ It is more flexible than it may seem. 'I' does not have to be you, or anyone like you. In 'Of Mice and Mistletoe' by Fabian Acker (in *Hoovering the Roof 2* by the East Dulwich Writers Group (Earwig Press)), the growing passion between a research scientist and one of his students is observed by one of their experimental animals. In the opening lines of 'Behind the Times' by Arthur Conan Doyle (one of his lesser-known, non-Sherlock Holmes stories; available in an audio book *The Beetle Hunter and Other Stories* (Crimson Cats – www.crimsoncats.co.uk)), the moment of birth is described from a first-person point of view – the first person being the baby.
- ▶ It can be intimate and emotionally intense. In the example quoted above, it invites identification with the narrator's plight as a reluctant house-mover.

- It allows for intrigue, uncertainty and plot development. The comment 'it was sure to be something obscene' comes solely from the narrator's point of view. There is no objective information about what the boy actually said, and the assumption that it was 'something obscene' may say more about the narrator than it does about the boy. The truth can emerge later.
- Being a participant in the action, the narrator may not be an entirely reliable witness, and this can be used to add edginess and irony to the story. Sometimes, the telling of the story can be part of the story itself. In Grace Paley's short story 'The Little Girl' (in her collection *Enormous Changes at the Last Minute* (Virago)), the first-person narrator has every reason to believe that two of his friends raped and murdered a teenage girl in his – the narrator's – flat. But the details of the crime are more horrific than he can bear, so he finds another way to tell the story, a version he can be more comfortable with.

Disadvantages of first person

- It sets limits to what can be told. Only those events which the narrator participates in, or witnesses, can be included in the story.
- It doesn't reveal much about the narrator – not their gender, not their looks, not even their name. Sooner or later, the author will have to find a way for the narrator to give enough personal details to let the reader know whose story this is.
- The author will have to work within the inevitable subjectivity of the I-narrator, and show to what extent their account can be relied upon.

2 SECOND PERSON

As you inserted the key into the lock, you were hoping it would stick. That would have allowed you to believe that it was the wrong key, the wrong lock, that you had come to the wrong house.

But the little Yale, with the estate agent's fob dangling from it, slid in smoothly and turned with ease. The door swung open. It was true, then. Of all the houses in all the world, you had bought this one.

You stepped inside. At the end of the path, two teenage boys passed. One of them made a remark that you did not catch. You guessed it was something obscene. You closed the door and locked it.

Advantages of second person

▶ It's unusual. See the work of Helen Dunmore for examples of how it can be done, in short stories and other forms. 'The Fag' and 'Be Vigilant, Rejoice, Eat Plenty' are in her short story collection *Ice Cream* (Viking). Her second-person poem 'The Malarkey' is available online.

▶ It can be spooky and unsettling. Even though the story is addressed to 'you', there is usually an 'I' present or implied. Is the 'you' character being stalked by someone who is not only watching them, but reading their mind and silently talking to them? Is the reader conspiring with the stalker?

▶ Second person is flexible. The 'you' can be a specific person, or people in general. The 'you' might be the narrator, talking to herself, or with multiple personalities. The narrator might be talking to someone who cannot reply, because they are dead or asleep or comatose, imaginary or gagged. They may be a new-born baby; or someone whose professional role is not to reply but to listen – a therapist, a confessor, an interrogator. The narrator may be confiding in 'you' the reader, or giving instructions. (In 'How to Tell a True War Story' by Tim O'Brien, in his collection *The Things They Carried* (Flamingo), the narrator tells several war stories, interspersed with tips on how to tell them. The tips are addressed to 'you'.) Or the use of 'you' might be a distancing device, a way for the narrator to avoid intense emotion by pretending that what happened didn't happen to them. 'You don't expect to have to bury your own child. They're supposed to bury you. That's the natural order. But sometimes the natural order gets it wrong and then it's you that has to make the arrangements, you that has choose the coffin…'

Disadvantages of second person

▶ It is quite difficult to maintain.

▶ It is not always convincing, and can sometimes be irritating, to have a narrator telling another character things that they already know.

Insight

Second-person is probably the most difficult point of view for a short story writer to handle successfully. So give it a try, and see what you can make of it.

Yes, I mean you.

3 THIRD PERSON (ONE POINT OF VIEW)

> As the middle-aged woman in the sheepskin coat inserted the key into the lock, she was hoping it would stick. That would have allowed her to believe that it was the wrong key, the wrong lock, that she had come to the wrong house.
>
> But the little Yale, with the estate agent's fob dangling from it, slid in smoothly and turned with ease. The door swung open. It was true, then. Of all the houses in all the world, Vicky Sinclair had bought this one.
>
> She stepped inside. At the end of the path, two teenage boys passed. One of them made a remark that she didn't catch. She guessed that it was something obscene. She closed the door and locked it.

Advantages of third person (one point of view)

▶ It is similar to first person, with most of the corresponding advantages.

▶ It allows you to name the character, describe them from an external point of view and say something about their state of mind, without the self-consciousness that comes from doing this in the first person. Elizabeth Taylor's 'Tall Boy', in her collection *The Devastating Boys* (Virago), describes a couple of days in the life of Jasper, a new immigrant to London. The story is told in the third person, but as no point of view is explored other than Jasper's, the story maintains a sort of aching intimacy as Jasper lives out his lonely life, and tries to make friends. He is described from an external point of view – 'he was a tall, slender young man, and his eyes had always looked mournful, even when he was happier, though hungry, at home in his own country.' Apart from that, all the thoughts and perceptions in the story are his own. There are other characters, but they are perceived through him. There is never any doubt whose story this is.

Disadvantages of third person (one point of view)

▶ What it gains in flexibility, when compared with the first person, it may lose in intimacy and directness.

4 THIRD PERSON (MORE THAN ONE POINT OF VIEW)

> As Vicky Sinclair inserted the key into the lock, she was hoping it would stick. That would have allowed her to believe that it was the wrong key, the wrong lock, that she had come to the wrong house.

But the little Yale, with the estate agent's fob dangling from it, slid in smoothly and turned with ease. The door swung open. It was true, then. Of all the houses in all the world, she had bought this one.

Vicky stepped inside. At the end of the path, Jack and Sam Vance passed, on their way home from school. At breakfast that morning, their mother had said something about No. 73 having been sold, and how she hoped the new people wouldn't be like their predecessors, the Bleasdales, with their rowdy behaviour and dirty habits. To Jack, the new woman didn't look the party type – the miserable old cow didn't even reply when he called out 'Afternoon!' She just glared at him and slammed the door.

Advantages of third person (more than one point of view)
▶ It's flexible, allowing both writer and reader to move back and forth between different characters.
▶ It gives more information: the boys' names, and Jack's thoughts, which could not be known by Vicky, are available to the reader.
▶ It gives a different angle on what Vicky thought she heard, showing her in a different light. In the first-person account, she seemed like a vulnerable woman under verbal attack from a passing stranger; this would have engaged the reader's sympathy. Now that sympathy is reduced by the discovery that the stranger was trying to be friendly, yet she was ready to think the worst of him.
▶ By recounting what Jack's mother said at breakfast about the previous occupants of the house, this approach introduces other characters and opens up ways for the story to develop.

Disadvantages of third person (more than one point of view)
▶ It requires consistency. Having allowed your reader to see once into the mind of Jack Vance, you need to develop him as a character, just as you need to develop all your point-of-view characters. You can't be in their minds one minute, and, the next, building plots on the basis that the reader doesn't know what they are thinking. It is possible to write a short story from several different points of view simultaneously, but this has to be done in accordance with a plan, not randomly. Maeve Binchy's story 'Murmurs in Montrose', in her collection *Dublin 4* (Arrow Books), uses seven different points of view to show what happens when Gerry Moore comes out of the nursing

home where he has been treated for alcoholism. Each of the point-of-view characters is fully developed; each has a different relationship with Gerry and a different attitude to his drinking. In Binchy's hands, this approach works magnificently, but it's a formidable task, and perhaps not one to be undertaken lightly by a newcomer to short story writing.

▶ With a wandering point of view, it is not always clear who can be believed. While this can be used creatively, it can also be confusing. What are we, the readers, supposed to think about the Bleasdales, when all we know is what a teenage boy remembers his mother (whom we haven't even met) saying about them at breakfast?

5 OMNISCIENT

Moving house is known to be one of life's most stressful events, and so it was for Vicky Sinclair on the day she took possession of 73 Gloucester Terrace. As she inserted the key into the lock, she was hoping it would stick. That would have allowed her to believe that it was the wrong key, the wrong lock, that she had come to the wrong house.

Sadly it was a vain hope. 73 Gloucester Terrace was hers whether she liked it or not; she had signed the papers and handed over the cash. Two miles away, Mr Ellis Ecclestone, like the typical estate agent he was, was rubbing his hands and counting his commission, unconcerned that Vicky, like many new home-owners, was convinced that she had made a terrible mistake.

She stepped inside. At the end of the path, Jack and Sam Vance were passing, on their way home from school. 'They've arrived then,' said Jack. Sam grunted. The two of them were not that interested in who the new neighbours were, but their mother was. She was dreading a repetition of the Bleasdales – ASBO material, the lot of them. Jack called out 'Afternoon' but Vicky did not reply, just closed the door and gazed disconsolately round her new home.

Advantages of omniscient point of view
▶ It does what it says: it knows everything, including what is going on in the minds of people in a different place.
▶ It allows for a fast-moving, crowded, action-packed narrative.

▶ It allows the author to comment, joke, generalize and editorialize from a distance. In 'The Bolt behind the Blue' by Dorothy Parker (in *The Collected Dorothy Parker* (Penguin)), a story of an uneasy friendship between a wealthy woman and a poor one, we move between the points of view of the two women, seeing in each case how her bank balance and social status influences her perceptions of the other. Meanwhile, a sardonically omniscient narrator, who doesn't like either of the women very much, hovers, watches and comments.

Disadvantages of omniscient point of view

▶ As with the third person using more than one point of view, it demands that the writer develop and manage several different characters at once, a difficult (though not impossible) feat.

▶ If the omniscient narrator comments subjectively on the action (as this one does: 'moving house is known to be one of life's most stressful events' 'like the typical estate agent he was'), sooner or later, the reader will start to wonder whose subjectivity this is. The author must decide whether the omniscient narrator is a participant in the action (in which case she/he ceases to be omniscient), or is a distant figure, godlike, editorial, sociological – and perhaps rather irritating.

Insight

Use omniscient narrators only with extreme caution. No one likes a know-all.

Those are your main options, when it comes to point of view. None of them is inherently better or worse than the others – all have their pros and cons, all can work well or fall flat on their faces. Each has its advocates and brilliant practitioners, as well as writers who avoid that approach. But there is little doubt that some are easier than others for the newcomer to manage: most notably first person, and third person from one point of view. So stick with them for a while.

If you find yourself chafing against the limitations of these approaches, try instead to see them as a creative opportunity. The fact that you can't state what a particular character is thinking (because the story is not told from his or her point of view) means that you must show it by words and behaviour, as perceived by your narrator or point-of-view character. You can't say 'he was feeling sick', but you can show how he looked and behaved. (Did he turn pale? Retch? Avert his eyes from the plate of greasy food in front of him?) You can't include events that your point-of-view character has not witnessed, but you can look for ways of reporting them, through documents or dialogue or clues.

By choosing a limited point of view, you have deprived yourself of some material. But you have given yourself something equally important. By reducing your range of alternatives, you have helped yourself along the route towards qualities that a short story must have: tightness, economy and, above all, intensity.

10 THINGS TO TRY

1 Go to the consumer page in a newspaper where readers send in their hard-luck stories – they were forced to pay an unjust surcharge on a train, they found meat in a 'vegetarian' dish in a restaurant, their five-star holiday hotel had a pile of rubble in the swimming pool. The newspaper's campaigning journalists step in, unmask the bad guy, and put things right. Choose one of these stories and retell it in the first person from the point of view of the bad guy, who, in his version, isn't actually a bad guy at all – just an ordinary bloke trying to do his job.

2 Write a second-person account of a day in the life of a seriously ill child. The narrator is one of the child's parents, who, speaking to the child in the silence of their mind, says the things that they dare not say out loud.

3 Write about a dental appointment from the point of view of the dentist. (If you happen to be a dentist, write it from the point of view of the patient.)

4 Write about walking through snow, from the point of view of someone who is warmly clad and has a centrally heated home to go to.

5 Write about walking through snow, from the point of view of someone who is homeless.

6 Write a story called 'Missing Person', from the point of view of an omniscient narrator who knows where the missing person is.

7 Write about a terrorist incident from the point of view of the terrorist.

8 A couple lie awake in bed, each believing that the other is asleep. Write a first-person inner monologue for each of them, then combine it into a single story, alternating the points of view between paragraphs. Use typefaces and spacing to show whose thoughts are whose.

9 Write a story about someone's first day in prison, told by their cellmate who has been there for ten years.

10 Write a first person account of the first hour of being dead, from the point of view of the dead person.

5

Intensity

In this chapter, you will learn:
- *how to add intensity to your stories*
- *how to let your readers find themselves in your story*
- *the importance of choosing the right word and the right image*
- *the importance of showing rather than telling.*

The experience of reading your story should be intense and memorable for the reader. The story should stay with them for a long time – like a special kiss, like a delicacy, like a tune in the head, like toothache.

How to achieve intensity

We've seen that you should make a clear and thoughtful decision on point of view, and stick with it. You, as writer, should know exactly whose story this is. Let the reader know, too.

A strong and effective concentration on the point-of-view character's perceptions and feelings will, even if these are flawed or incomplete, evoke the intensity of the reader's own experiences, their inner landscape, their hopes and fears, their memories – which may also be flawed and incomplete. Even if the reader has never been in the situation described in the story, or anything like it, they will start to imagine it.

Insight

'Readers used to speak of "losing" themselves in a novel or a story: the contemporary addict turns to the short story to find himself.' (V.S. Pritchett, Introduction to *The Oxford Book of Short Stories* (Oxford University Press))

My shelves, and probably yours too, are full of books of short stories which we have kept because each volume contains at least one story to which we return again and again for the frisson of recognition: that moment of thinking, yes, I've been there, I've thought that, done that, or I wish I had – or I fear that, given the same set of circumstances, I might behave in the same unfortunate way. This applies even when the author is from an era, a part of the world, a social group or a culture that is a long way from our own.

How have they achieved this?

Their chosen form has helped. The short story is uniquely well suited to the quick observation, the passing remark, the barely mentioned incident which, in a novel, might demand development and so, in the wrong hands, lose edge and accuracy.

Insight

A story works because the author gives the impression of having read the reader's mind. In fact, the author has read only her own, pinpointing a moment of common humanity, in which the reader recognizes himself.

In Emily Prager's short story set in thirteenth-century China 'A Visit from the Footbinder' (in her collection *A Visit from the Footbinder* (Chatto & Windus)), six-year-old Pleasure Mouse eagerly awaits her rite of passage into womanhood, only to discover that, once the procedure has been performed, she, who only hours ago was skipping and dancing, can now not even walk without excruciating pain. When I read it, I immediately recognized my six-year-old self, who, half a world away and seven centuries later, thought going into hospital for a few days to have my tonsils out might be a bit of a lark, but woke up after the operation unable to speak or swallow.

Look for yourself in the short stories that you read. Even if the encounter is an uncomfortable one, it shows that the author knew what he was doing when he wrote the story in that way. Short story writers achieve this effect not by generalizing about huge concepts, such as the human race or the meaning of life or love. They do it by thinking small, by writing about small moments, small objects which cast long shadows. Pleasure Mouse squeezes water chestnuts in her hands to distract her from the agony of her mutilated feet; I, with my sore throat, was given a plastic parrot which squawked when you pressed a button.

The short story achieves intensity by reaching out from the specificity of its content, to the generality of human experience. Tadeusz Borowski's 'This Way for the Gas, Ladies and Gentlemen', in the *Penguin Book of International Short Stories,* looks closely and unflinchingly at day-to-day life in a Nazi concentration camp. The more horrific his observations, the more they become almost cosy, almost domestic, as the mind struggles to accommodate them. Inmates' clothes are washed in Zyklon B, the same substance used to kill people, because it is equally effective at killing lice. The repeated arrival of freight trucks full of new victims is like 'a late showing of the same film'. It's as if we have all been there.

> Try this
> **Identify the most frightening situation** in which you have ever found yourself. Identify a single small object which you associate with that predicament. **Describe it.** Put a fictional character into the same predicament, and put the object into their hand.
> **Now write the story.**

Some dos and don'ts

What other strategies can you use to give your stories intensity – the sort of intensity that allows a stranger 'find themselves' in your world?

CHOOSE YOUR WORDS AND IMAGES WITH CARE AND PRECISION

At the end of Tim O'Brien's short story 'Nogales' (published in *The New Yorker*, 8 March 1999), a middle-aged woman named Karen is abandoned in a desert without food, water or shade, by a couple of drug smugglers about whom she knows too much. The cruelty of the fate she faces is huge, as is the desert, and Karen herself is quite a large woman. But O'Brien encapsulates her predicament in a single small image: the sensation in her mouth of 'a little bud of thirst'.

It's that three-letter word 'bud' that does it. Buds are usually perceived as tiny, innocent things, with potential for flowering into prettiness or magnificence. This one contains only horror. It is inside the mouth of someone we have come to know, and it is growing. As an image it is unforgettable.

You don't have to have been abandoned to die of exposure in a desert to appreciate and shudder at Karen's fate. You need only to know the sensation of having a dry mouth.

Other sensations can be perceived through sight, sound, taste and smell – or the absence of these. In 'My Vocation' by Mary Lavin (in *The Oxford Book of Short Stories*, edited by V.S. Pritchett), the 13-year-old female narrator, who is thinking of becoming a nun, announces that she loves the way nuns smell. Her father reproaches her for suggesting that they smell at all, and she realizes that they don't: in her overcrowded, teeming street in a Dublin slum, nuns are the only people who are without smell.

Insight

A smell, a sound, a taste, a sight or the feel of something may be vivid, startling – or incongruously absent. The absence of a sense impression may be a sense impression in itself.

Try this
Describe:

- a sound that you associate with the head teacher of the first school you attended
- the smell of Sunday morning in the street where you live
- the first thing you notice about your face when you look in a mirror
- the taste of love
- the sensation of putting on brand-new underwear.

Now choose one of these sensations, the one that you think you have described most intensely. Give it to a fictional character, someone quite unlike you: much older, much younger, of a different different nationality or different gender. **Write a story that has this sensation at its centre.**

DON'T TRY TO TELL EVERYTHING

We are talking about *short* stories. If you try to pack too much in, you may lose the intensity of a concentrated, focused narrative.

Suppose you want to write a story about a family – yours or someone else's, real or imagined. Don't include everybody. Choose just one family member and write about him, about one thing that he did, one thing that happened to him.

Get in close: tell it from the point of view of the character you are most interested in, and in whom you want your reader to take most interest. Let other family members hang about in the background or make occasional interventions, but keep your eye, and the reader's eye (and ear, and heart, and hope, and anxiety) on that one person. That is a way to achieve intensity. It may also, if well handled, give a much stronger impression of the family as a whole than if you had set out deliberately to pack in everyone as main players in the story.

GET IT RIGHT

If your story contains material that is factual and verifiable, verify it. Few things can be more effective at breaking into the intensity of a story, than for a reader to realize that the author has got something wrong.

DON'T LECTURE, OR POINT OUT MORALS

Perhaps you have a political or moral purpose in writing: you want to write a story about the urgency of protecting the environment, or the evils of racism, or the importance of gender equality. Good for you. But don't make the mistake of taking on the whole issue – that is a job for a manifesto or pamphlet, not a short story. Instead, write the story of one person coughing their way through a cloud of traffic fumes, or living in a threatened community. Write the story of one person suffering racism or sexism, or – perhaps more challengingly – one person who has a racist or sexist view of the world. Let them have it. Write the story. Let the politics take care of themselves. They will, if the story you have written has enough intensity.

Try this
Write a love story. But don't try to make it about love as a whole. It's too big. Don't even try to make it about one love affair. Most of those are too big as well. Write a story about one encounter between two lovers.
Then write another story about one lover alone.

A **simile** is a figure of speech in which one thing is compared with another: it usually takes the form 'as... as' or 'like...'

> *His face was as white as a sheet.*

This says more than just 'his face was white' because the reader will know what a white sheet looks like, and know how shocking and out-of-place that sort of whiteness would be in a person's face.

> *The lump in her breast was small and hard, like a frozen pea.*

This not only reveals dimensions of the lump, but it gives an added note of the sinister by equating it with a foodstuff. And the word 'frozen' evokes both fear and death.

A **metaphor** is an implied simile: a statement which, though not intended to be taken as literally true, evokes a comparison and creates a strong mental image:

> *She was incandescent with rage.*

Similes and metaphors can be effective ways of adding intensity to the descriptions (of people, places, things, incidents) in your stories. But they can have the opposite effect if they are not used precisely. A recent report on an earthquake included the comment that 'the survivors are suffering from a cocktail of terror'. What the speaker presumably had in mind is that a cocktail is a mixture of different ingredients, and the earthquake survivors had a mixture of different things to be terrified of. But a cocktail is a pleasant thing, not generally a source of terror, so 'cocktail of terror' is nonsense. Far from adding intensity or vividness, this metaphor distracts from what could just as easily, and much more effectively, have been expressed in the simple statement 'the survivors have many fears'.

Some mixed or misused metaphors, far from adding intensity, merely make themselves ridiculous: 'Another milestone tumbles!' exclaimed a sports commentator about an athlete who had completed a run in the fastest-ever time. 'Nobody is going to have women bishops forced down their throat,' said a senior cleric in a recent speech.

Before committing yourself to a metaphor, ask yourself: what picture does this create in the reader's mind? Is it the picture you intend, and will it add intensity to the reader's imagined perception of what you are trying to describe? If not, abandon the metaphor and write in plain, literal English.

If you are comparing one thing with something else, be sure that you know what the quality is that they have in common. Be sure, too, that it applies to both of them, and that your intended reader is familiar with both. There's not much point in saying 'the model's legs were as thin as pipe cleaners' to an audience that has never seen a pipe cleaner.

SHOW, DON'T TELL

'Don't tell me the moon is shining,' wrote the Russian short story writer Anton Chekhov. 'Show me the glint of light on broken glass.'

You can extend that principle:

▶ Don't tell your reader that the hospital was unhygienic: show the soiled dressing abandoned under the bed. Go for the evocative detail that makes the reader go 'yuk', not the big, bland generalization that sounds like something out of an official report.
▶ Don't tell the reader that the dog is ferocious: show it taking a bite out of the hand of the dinner party guest.
▶ Don't tell the reader that the error message that came up on the computer was incomprehensible: reproduce it. Let the reader share the bafflement and annoyance. (Alternatively, let the reader feel superior because she understands the error message perfectly.)

By showing rather than telling, you invite the reader to share the experience, which is always more intense than simply being told about it.

INCLUDE A MOMENT OF EPIPHANY

In religion and mythology, 'epiphany' signifies an encounter with a god or goddess. In a literary context, it tends to mean an intense moment of realization, a moment of truth.

Raymond Carver used to keep a card on his desk containing a quotation from Chekhov: '...and suddenly everything became clear to him.' Carver found these words 'full of wonder and possibility.' ('A Storyteller's Shoptalk', *New York Times*, 15 February 1981).

Let your character have a moment in which everything suddenly becomes clear. It could be:

▶ being converted to a cause – or losing faith
▶ falling in love with someone – or realizing that love has died
▶ the discovery of a betrayal – or an act of generosity
▶ a moment of guilt – or freedom from it
▶ the moment when someone realizes that they hate their job and have to leave – not at the end of the month, not this evening, but *now*.

Your reader will almost certainly have experienced at least one of those moments. It might have been ten years ago, or it might have been yesterday. Your task is to make him or her recognize that moment – and themselves – in your story. Ask yourself what, in precise terms, led to the epiphany. Was it one event, or a sequence? Was it something somebody said or did? Focus on the smallness of the moment. Describe it with such precision, honesty and intensity that the reader cannot fail to recognize it.

Try this
What is your most embarrassing secret? Write a short story about a fictional character who does what you did. (Make a deal with yourself before you start that you will *never* tell anyone that the story is about you. Without this assurance, you may be too inhibited to write honestly about it.)

Somewhere among your readership there may be someone who has the same secret as you – or another one, the memory of which induces similar unease. Finding themselves in your story will be an intense and unforgettable experience for them. You may even end up in their desert island story collection.

10 THINGS TO KEEP IN MIND

1 The events in your stories will be experienced intensely by the characters. (If they are not, why are you writing a story about them?) Share that intensity with your readers.

2 Remember to choose a point of view and stick with it. (If you are unsure on this point, have another look at Chapter 4.)

3 Look for yourself in the short stories of other authors. If you find yourself, try to identify how the author – who has probably never met you – has managed to put you there.

4 Let your reader find himself/herself in your stories.

5 Don't use metaphors and similes just to make yourself look clever, or your writing more 'writerly'. Use them because they add intensity to your reader's experience of the story. If they don't do this, leave them out and use plain English.

6 If your story has a moral, keep quiet about it. Either it will reveal itself in your story, or it's not there – and sticking it on at the end won't help.

7 Show, don't tell.

8 Favour the specific over the general.

9 An intense moment of realization, or epiphany, can be both moving and exciting for the reader.

10 If your story makes your reader feel uncomfortable – congratulations.

6

Enjoy

In this chapter, you will learn:
- *how to enjoy writing short stories (at least some of the time)*
- *how to enjoy reading short stories (at least some of the time)*
- *how to read as a writer.*

By now you should have quite a few short stories in your life that weren't there before you started reading this book: the ones you have written in response to the exercises, and the ones you have read in response to the recommendations.

Did you enjoy them? Are you enjoying the fact of having written them, and read them?

Let's hope so. As a storyteller and a lover of stories, you are taking part in an activity that is as old as human communication, and as important. Short stories have their origins in the oral tradition. The human attention span is only just so long, so the teller of tales in a cave or by a campfire or on a long march will have had to learn to keep things short and focused, memorable and absorbing.

Then as now, stories will have done many things: they will have amused and informed, reassured and warned. Stories bring order to a disordered universe. Even if that order is only an illusion, it may, like other forms of entertainment, be a comfort or a welcome distraction. Stories pass on cultural values, or challenge them. They remind us of who we are, and who we could be.

Insight

One thing short stories probably won't do for you is make you lots of money. So you might as well enjoy them for their own sake.

We have already seen some of the steps you can take to create a writing environment for yourself that will welcome you to work – somewhere private and comfortable, with plenty of treats and assignments, and the minimum of distractions.

Enjoy the sense of being a worker in the world of literature. Of choosing the words that say exactly what you mean. Of watching those words spreading across the screen, your plots unfolding on the page.

Warming up

It won't always be like that. There are times when they don't spread and don't unfold. There are times writers hate writing, mainly because we think we can't do it. We're stuck, and it hurts. What then?

We can give up, of course – temporarily or even permanently. But that is an extreme remedy. Try some of these warm-up exercises first:

- What is your name? Who chose it? Why? Write the story behind your name.
- BBC Radio created a series called *A History of the World in 100 Objects*. Do the same for your own life – or at least make a start.
- Remember an argument you had when the other person got the better of you. By the time you realized what you should have said, it was too late. Rewrite the argument, giving yourself all the best lines.
- Find a hat – any hat, your own or someone else's. Put it on, and don't take it off until you have written a story about it.
- Look at a photograph of a social gathering involving your family. Who wasn't there? Why not? Write the story of the absentee.
- Write down a joke you've heard and liked. Chances are it was a well-told story. Let it lead you to create another one.

Insight

'I'm really looking forward to the summer,' said a university professor to a friend who writes for a living. 'I'm going to relax in the garden and write stories.'

'Sounds great,' the writer replied. 'I'm going to relax in my garden and become a university professor.'

Only non-writers imagine that authors sit in an effort-free trance while their story descends from the skies in a beam of light. People who actually do it know that it is work. Special work.

The writer Susan Hill has said that she 'can't stand those writers who make a fuss. I mean, you don't have to do it. I just can't understand this "it's all so difficult" business. Yes, I love it, and I can't be bothered with "it's such agony". That is so pretentious.' (Interview in *The Observer*, 16 January 2011.)

Stella Duffy, by contrast, says that it always surprises her when she hears of writers saying they like writing – 'I don't, and neither do most of the published writers I know. I like having written.' But she acknowledges that 'writers are fortunate to have an occupation that we are happy with. We work hard, but it is not hard work in the way some factory work is hard, and cleaning someone else's house is hard. Even if we are only making a tiny amount of money from writing, we are lucky to be able to play and enjoy it' (interview in *UK Writer*, autumn 2009, and conversation).

Is it 'play' to you? Is it hard work, or working hard? Or is it more like a habit or an addiction? It can be all of the above, as well as a craft, an art, a comfort, a profession, a vocation and a contribution towards your own immortality as a participant in the vital and uniquely human work of literature.

Reading as a writer

Speaking of literature – do you like short stories? Do you positively enjoy reading them?

Have you got plenty of short story collections on your shelves at home? Do you subscribe to short story magazines, or read short fiction on the Internet? When you visit bookshops and libraries, do you select short stories – at least some of the time – in preference to novels and non-fiction?

Do you listen to short stories on the radio or on podcasts or CDs? Do you attend short story reading events? If your daily newspaper has a short story supplement, do you consider it a bonus? At meetings of your writing group, do you get as much pleasure from hearing other members' short stories as you do from presenting your own? Can you think of eight short stories which, if you were to be cast away alone on a desert island, you would choose to have with you?

Here (in no particular order) are mine:

- ▶ 'Witching Hour' by Sally Hinchcliffe (in *Tales of the Decongested*, vol. 1, edited by Rebekah Lattin-Rawstrone and Paul Blaney (Apis Books))
- ▶ 'The Adventure of the Speckled Band' by Arthur Conan Doyle (available online – Google the title)
- ▶ 'The Hanging Girl' by Ali Smith (in her collection *Other Stories and Other Stories* (Penguin))
- ▶ 'Crepuscule' by Can Themba (in his collection *The Will to Die* (Heinemann))
- ▶ 'Polaris' by Fay Weldon (in her collection *Polaris and Other Stories* (Coronet))
- ▶ 'Trespassing' by Valerie Miner (in her collection *Trespassing and Other Stories* (Methuen))
- ▶ 'It Came in a Box' by Stella Duffy (in *The New English Library Book of Internet Stories*, edited by Maxim Jakubowski)
- ▶ 'Fat' by Raymond Carver (in *The Penguin Book of International Short Stories, 1945–1985*, edited by Daniel Halpern).

Try this

Identify your desert island short stories. Write your list quickly. Don't think about it too much. It's not your last word on the subject – you can change your choices tomorrow, just as I will probably change mine. Don't worry about being even-handed, or showing the breadth of your literary knowledge: there is a time and a place for that, but it's not what you are doing now. You are simply trying to identify what you like, the stories you return to again and again, either for old, familiar pleasures, or because you know you will always find something of yourself in them, or something else that you didn't notice before.

It might be to do with **the spooky sadness of the tale,** as was the case for me with Ali Smith's 'The Hanging Girl', or the sheer visceral nastiness of Arthur Conan Doyle's story of murder-by-snakebite, 'The Adventure of the Speckled Band'. It might be **the way the story teases you:** Sally Hinchcliffe's 'Witching Hour' tells of a group of faintly ridiculous people being taken in by a conman, but it doesn't allow its readers to feel too superior, if we were taken in, too.

It might be **the interaction of the personal and the political** – Can Themba's 'Crepuscule', a tale of interracial romance and survival in apartheid South Africa, shows the liveliness, fortitude, folly and sexiness of human beings who never give up in the quest for love. It might be **the different takes on subject matter close to your heart:** Fay Weldon's 'Polaris' and Raymond Carver's 'Fat' both contain people who are, in their different ways, obsessed with food. It might be the **contrast between cosiness and danger** in Valerie Miner's 'Trespassing'. Or it might be the mixture of **outrage and fascination** aroused by the story's subject – in Stella Duffy's 'It Came in a Box', a woman who wants a man decides to order one from the Internet – piece by piece.

It might be none of those things. Your desert island stories will be different from mine. The point is that you enjoy them and want to keep them with you.

If I could see your list, I would be interested but not too bothered by what was on it: whether the stories were all from one genre or even by one author, or whether they come from all over the world, from the mainstream or literature's outer fringes. My only concern would be if you couldn't come up with any titles at all, as that would suggest that you don't have much enthusiasm for reading short stories. And if you don't enjoy reading them, why do you want to write them?

One possible answer is that you've read all the short stories you want to read, and they were all rubbish. You have decided to do the genre a favour by writing some decent ones. This somewhat-less-than-modest approach does at least have the merit of suggesting that you have read a lot of short stories, if only to discover how bad they are. Which is better than not reading them at all.

But it doesn't answer the question of how your short stories are to be published. To get published, a story has to arouse the enthusiasm of a publisher, and it does that by giving the publisher the impression that it will arouse the enthusiasm of readers. If you have no such enthusiasm yourself, how do you expect to impart it to others?

Insight

If your ambition is to write short stories and get them published, read the work of people who have already done both these things.

Which short stories should you read?

There are four possible answers to this. Choose the one that suits you. Over time, you could do all four.

1 READ AT RANDOM

It doesn't matter which short stories you read as long as you read plenty. A short story is complete in itself, so you don't have to read them in any particular order. Start with whatever you've got on your shelves at home. Move on to your local library and bookshops. Ask the staff to alert you when new short story collections are published, whether by the large publishers, or small community presses. When you find a collection that appeals to you, *buy it if you possibly can.* Better yet, buy it from a small, independent bookshop. (I know you're not made of money, but when your short stories are published, you'll be hoping people will buy them, won't you? And you'll be hoping that there will still be bookshops to buy them from.)

Keep an eye on short stories in magazines. You'll find a list, on the website www.theshortstory.org.uk, of nearly 80 magazines which publish short stories. Some, like *Ambit*, *Granta*, *Women's Weekly*, *Writers' Forum* and *MsLexia*, are long-established. Others come and go.

Search the shelves of second-hand bookshops and charity shops for short story collections, the ones by household name authors, and the ones by people you have never heard of. Make friends with your heritage, your contemporaries, your peers, your rivals. Think of short fiction as a field, and graze in it.

2 TAKE A COURSE

If you prefer a more organized approach to your reading, then the second answer to the question of what you should be reading may be found in formal study. Check out your nearest university or adult education institution for courses on the history and theory of the short story, or more general literature courses that include short stories in the syllabus.

A word of caution: don't get so bogged down in literary criticism that you lose the will to write. Don't be so awed by your literary forebears that you feel unworthy to follow in their footsteps. No one is asking you to follow in anyone's footsteps; aim instead to create some footsteps of your own.

Insight

If literary theory helps you with your writing, then by all means study it. But don't let theory get in the way of practice.

None of this is said to belittle literary criticism, or to deny the obvious fact that the skills of the writer and the skills of the literary critic often coexist in the same person. One fine example is the novelist David Lodge, whose book *The Art of Fiction*, written in clear, accessible language, uses specific examples from existing literature to teach writing skills.

Creative writing and literary criticism are not the same. Literary criticism is a response to texts, but, before texts can be responded to, they have to be brought into existence. That is the writer's job.

3 DEVISE A COURSE OF YOUR OWN

If you don't want to go to classes, you could devise a course of your own. Read at least one or two stories by acknowledged masters and mistresses of the short story form, for example:

Sir Walter Scott	Katharine Mansfield	Raymond Carver
Ivan Turgenev	Virginia Woolf	V.S. Pritchett
Guy de Maupassant	D.H. Lawrence	Bessie Head
Edgar Alan Poe	Ernest Hemingway	Angela Carter
Anton Chekhov	Dorothy Parker	A.L. Kennedy
H.G. Wells	Franz Kafka	Ali Smith

(You can add your own favourites to this list.)

Read everything in *The Penguin Book of International Short Stories, 1945–1985*, including the introduction by Daniel Halpern. And read William Boyd's article 'A Short History of the Short Story', first published in *Prospect* magazine in July 2006, and available online. Read at least one story by each of the authors Boyd mentions.

That's a lot of reading, and I am not suggesting you do it all at once. I am certainly not suggesting that you let it get in the way of your writing. Spread it over your lifetime.

4 READ THE STORIES MENTIONED THROUGHOUT THIS BOOK

These are not simply recommendations, made in the spirit of 'read this, it's important' or even 'you'll enjoy it'. They are presented as examples of how a particular author has shown a particular skill, dealt with a particular writing issue.

Don't read passively, or solely as an audience. Read as a writer, as a craftsperson. Be aware of how the story has been put together, and whether it works.

Which point of view has the writer chosen to write from? Was it a good choice? Note the effect the story has on you – does it make you laugh or cry, feel sick or sexy or hungry or angry or wistful, does it remind you of something or somebody? How has the author achieved this? What can you learn from that achievement, and use in your own stories?

You won't enjoy all the stories equally, or even at all. When you read as a writer you are allowed to have favourites. You are also allowed to be bored to tears by people whose work everyone else seems to admire. Even the also-rans can teach you something. If you find yourself flicking through the pages to see how much longer a story is going to drag on, try to identify the point at which your interest started to flag.

Insight

When reading short stories, think of yourself as an apprentice in a workshop. Look over the shoulders of more experienced authors, and pay attention to what they are doing. Would you have done it that way? Why, or why not?

The experience of reading a good short story has been compared with being tapped on the shoulder and told a secret, or accidentally opening an intimate letter that was meant for someone else, or finding a message in a bottle. It's a quick insight into another world, it's startling, it's disconcerting, it's over almost as soon as it has begun, but it satisfies, intrigues or irritates with sufficient strength to stay with you. It may be like something glimpsed out of the corner of the eye, or seen through a lit-up window from a dark street. Less cosily, it may be like a slap in the face, or it may evoke Anne Enright's comment on Raymond Carver's short story 'Fat': 'The entry wound is so small, you could say, and the result so deadly' ('Twelve Tales for Christmas', *The Guardian*, 13 December 2010).

The difference between a short story and a novel has been equated with the difference between a string quartet and an orchestra, a lyric poem and an epic, a 100-metre dash and a marathon. Very short stories are known as flash fiction, paragraph fiction, postcard fiction, mini-sagas. Short stories may be experienced as slices of life, or vertical sections. Longer ones may be as complex and multifaceted as novels.

Which of these images, metaphors or comparisons best evokes your experience of reading your favourite short story will depend on the story and what you bring to the reading of it. It will depend on whether you find yourself in it.

Insight

Read a story that looks as if it might suit your mood – because of its title, or a word or passage that catches your eye. Go for it because it fits into your life. Taxi drivers read short stories when waiting for the next fare. Mothers of young babies read short stories when breastfeeding. Text messagers, bloggers, tweeters and Facebook friends sometimes put their gadgets away and read a short story instead.

Read a short story when you wake up in the morning, and another before you go to sleep at night. Listen to short stories on the radio, especially BBC Radio 3 and Radio 4, or www.shortstoryradio.com. If you share your home or your bed with another short story enthusiast, listen together. Or take turns to read a short story to each other. Enjoy short stories as audio books and podcasts. You can Google 'Short Story Audio Books' and 'Short Story Podcasts' to find out what's available: Crimson Cats (www.crimsoncats.co.uk), for example, has early stories by Jane Austen, and stories by Arthur Conan Doyle which do not feature Sherlock Holmes.

Go to short story events at literature festivals and in bookshops and libraries. Liars' League (www.liarsleague.typepad.com) is a short story event held in pubs.

Read a short story on your way to work, in your breaks, or, in the evenings, before you switch the television on, or go online. Read as a writer. Read as a fan.

10 THINGS TO KEEP IN MIND

1 Write for pleasure. Take pleasure in writing. If you can't manage that, then at least take pleasure in having written.

2 Make space in your life for reading short stories, and for listening to them on the radio or on audiobooks and podcasts.

3 Watch out for short story events in your area – literary festivals, authors giving readings in bookshops, and events in which you may be able to participate, such as Liars' League.

4 If you like a particular story, read it again. Try to identify what the author has done so successfully.

5 Take good care of your teeth. Dentists' waiting rooms are famous for stocking magazines that are not really your kind of thing, but which contain short stories that you might otherwise miss.

6 If you don't like one story in a magazine or collection, turn to another. Come back another day to the one you didn't like, and see whether, in a different mood, you like it any better.

7 Have favourites. Treasure them and learn from them.

8 Keep an eye on the book review pages of newspapers; be aware of who is writing new collections of short stories, or contributing to anthologies, and who is publishing them.

9 Make friends with your literary forebears. But don't feel you have to admire the work of author A because everyone else does, or avoid author B because he or she is generally considered too lowbrow. Make your own choices.

10 If you enjoy a short story by a contemporary author, write to them (c/o their publisher or website) and tell them so. You will make their day, and maybe one day someone will make yours in the same way.

7

Size matters

In this chapter, you will learn:
- *how short or long a short story can be*
- *how to write a story of a specified length*
- *approaches to writing very short stories*
- *approaches to writing longer short stories.*

The shortest story ever written is attributed to Ernest Hemingway:

> *For sale. Baby's jacket. Never worn.*

Others can be created using the same formula:

> *For sale. Wedding dress. Never worn.*

> *For sale. Child's drumkit. Unwanted gift.*

Here the substance of the stories lies in what is not said, but is clear nonetheless – the death of the baby, the cancellation of the wedding, the noise of the drums. Other very short stories, sometimes referred to as micro fiction, rest on an inner contradiction:

> *I used to be indecisive but now I'm not so sure.*

> *The lecture on clairvoyance has been cancelled, owing to unforeseen circumstances.*

> *Giving up smoking is easy – I've done it lots of times.*

> *I want to die peacefully in my sleep like my grandfather, not screaming with terror like his passengers.*

This sort of thing is popular with speech writers, and you can find plenty of examples online if you search for 'one-liners', 'six word stories', etc.

At the other end of the scale, Chekhov wrote stories of up to 30,000 words, some divided into chapters. When sold in collections, these tend to look like short stories but are, in fact, longer than some contemporary novels.

Insight

A short story is not a rigid literary form with a set length, like a sonnet or a haiku. The number of words depends on the author's preference, and the demands of the market.

If you are writing with a particular magazine, competition, website or radio slot in mind, make sure you know what length of story they are looking for. (See Chapter 18 for more information on this.) BBC Radio 4's 15-minute slot accommodates around 2,000 words. The Bridport Prize for flash fiction goes to a story of up to 250 words. *The Sunday Times* EFG Private Bank Short Story Award is for stories of up to 6,000 words. *Granta* magazine says it has no maximum or minimum length requirements, but points out that most of its submissions are between 3,000 and 6,000 words.

Once you know how many words are being looked for, *write to that length,* or, if it is a maximum, make sure you keep within it. Even if you don't have a particular market in mind at the moment, and are writing to please yourself, it is still a good mental discipline to set yourself a word-length and stick to it.

How to write a story of a particular length

First of all, here is how not to do it. Don't just scribble or tap away without restraint until you fear that you might have gone over the limit (or until your word-counter tells you that you definitely have), at which point you panic and write: 'He woke up and it was all a dream. THE END.' This approach is unlikely to be successful.

Nor is it a good idea to write a story that is much longer than the required length, and then start hacking it back for reasons of length alone. You may unbalance the story and lose something vital.

Insight

A short story should never read like an extract, a synopsis, or a piece off the cutting-room floor. Its brevity or length should be intrinsic to its subject matter and its appeal – not something imposed as an afterthought.

To write a story that will work out at a particular length, you need to think ahead.

Let us say that the length you are aiming at is 2,000 words. The first thing you need to know is: *what will 2,000 words – MY words – look like?*

The answer will vary between different writers, depending on the size of your handwriting or your chosen typeface, what sort of words you use, and how you set out your pages. Have a look at something else you have written, count the words, and work it out.

If 2,000 words means for you what it means for me, which is approximately six pages of A4, in double-spaced 12-point type, set those pages out in front of you. Get six sheets of blank A4 paper, put them on the table and make a mental image of them covered with your story.

At the top of page 1, imagine the beginning. Even if you have not yet started writing the story, imagine an opening scene, or a narrator's introductory comment. Feel the mood of the writing, get a sense of the reader being drawn in. At the end of page 6, imagine the end – the resolution, or the realization that there is no resolution.

Insight

Think of your story as a physical object: a fixed number of pages covered with text. Be aware at all times of how large or small the object is, and how close you are to the beginning, and to the end. This will help you to shape your story, and prevent you from using up all your words before you have told what you have to tell.

AN EXAMPLE

Let us suppose that you are writing a 2,000-word story about a seven-year-old child running away from abusive parents.

You start by showing the family's home life. Perhaps the parents are always drinking, and neglect the child's needs. There's pornography on the DVD player and tobacco smoke in the air, but no food on the table. The parents hit each other and hit the child. You describe several such incidents.

Suddenly you realize that you are halfway down page 5 and the child hasn't run away yet. He hasn't even started to think about it. That's what this story was supposed to be about, but, with only a page and a half to go, he is still in his own bed. You need to get him out of the house and en route for whatever fate awaits him.

So speed things up. Get him from his bed to the street in a line or two. Unless you've got some special difficulty in mind for him – someone hears him and tries to stop him, or he can't get the front door open – there is no need to go into a lot of detail: your readers know how easily a seven-year-old – neglected but determined – could leave a house. Once your protagonist is out on the dark street, you can revert to medium pace to describe an adventure he has, and give a flavour of what life is going to be like for him from now on.

That is one way of solving the problem of running out of words before you have told the story: speed things up. Another is to edit what has gone before: have another look at those first five pages which establish the child's home circumstances and the reasons for his flight, and consider what could be cut.

Insight

If your story needs to be shortened, it is often better to do it by removing whole incidents than by tweaking, editing or summarizing. Stories are about events. They need events, not case histories, synopses or sociological surveys.

If the child's mother and father are keener on the bottle than they are on their responsibilities as parents, don't think you can save space by generalizing about it: continue to show it in specific terms. But, whereas before you may have shown it in a sequence of incidents (that's how you came to use up those five and a half pages before you even got the child out of bed), you now confine yourself to one event. If it's the right event, and presented with enough intensity, it will say it all.

In an earlier chapter, we explored the importance of showing rather than telling. Follow that principle here. Don't tell the reader that the child is neglected. Instead, have him (for example) come downstairs one morning for breakfast and find there is no breakfast, only a vodka bottle, overflowing ashtrays and a glass, empty except for a twist of lemon. He's so hungry that he eats the lemon. Describe the taste of it on his tongue – the sourness of the fruit and the stale tang of the dregs of last night's booze. Trust that image to say everything that needs to be said about why he doesn't want to live here anymore. Then get him out of the house.

This sort of approach, as well as helping to bring you back to your intended word-length, can add pleasing tension to your story, and a creative unevenness to the pace of the narrative. This keeps the reader on the back foot, unsure of what is coming next but ready for it when it does. It allows you to draw maximum tension from brevity. But you won't be able to do this if you aren't aware *at all times* of how much of your allotted space you have used up, and what you have left. This applies whatever the length of your story.

Keeping it short

In time and with practice you will come to know almost by instinct how to vary your approach to a story, depending on how long it needs to be. Meanwhile, try these approaches.

FLASH FICTION

This term is generally used to mean stories of 200–500 words, the sort of length that would fit comfortably on a single page, or two facing pages, of a pocket-sized book and so could be read 'in a flash'. And the content should be startling – like a flash of lightning, or a sudden flash of insight.

What would a 250-word story look like in your writing? About a page? Imagine the story starting at the top and finishing at the bottom.

Insight

Flash fiction should make your reader blink.

Use a startling image, a bizarre event. Don't explain. Use a distinctive voice to tell what happened, then get out, leaving your reader dazzled. Have a look at 'The Butterfly Slippers' in Chapter 14 for an example of how this can work.

FIVE MINUTES

Another approach to keeping your stories short is to write a story called 'Five Minutes'. Write it to a length that will take five minutes to read aloud. (Probably between 700 and 800 words.)

Make the action of the story centre around a five-minute activity. (Evacuating a building in an emergency? Struggling with a duvet that won't go into its cover? Trying to get past a recalcitrant call centre operator to someone who can actually help? Fast sex?)

Keep an eye on the clock, and let at least one of your characters do the same. Let the reader worry about it, too. Use the passage of time to restrict your story, and so focus and energize it.

SMALL THINGS

To keep your story short, build it around a small object. Here's a 540-word story about something very small indeed:

Your Toe-Nail, by Victoria Rose Poolman

I found a toe nail clipping on the floor.

It was a great shard of nail, curved like a Beetle car bonnet. It was thick, too. And yellow – like custard made with too much milk. Most people would be disgusted … but I'm not: I think it's yours.

And when I hear of those cases on the news: little Madeline whom they never found, the murderer of that nice presenter lady, the DNA they discovered in his pocket, her bra, their car, I think of how much of *your* DNA I must have in my hand. Perhaps you could be recreated. Perhaps those doctors at Oxford who cloned that Dolly could somehow find your stem cells and your genes and implant the toenail into my womb and it would grow and grow and grow.

But then what if I gave birth to a giant toe nail?

I pulled the settee out last night. I pulled up the carpet. I tore off some wallpaper. And it took us so long to find that kind. But I was only looking – for you. When I thought about it, I remembered the eyelashes we put in your hair for wishes. They must have fallen here somewhere. I know there must be splinters that stuck in you, that tasted you, that must be here too. I had hoped there might be a tissue down the back of the chair, maybe you had cried when you first found out, and had wiped it away and stuffed it there out of laziness. Even if it's just a snotty one, that's fine.

I've grown to love the dust. It's all your skin and hair and loveliness falling and floating out of the sky like beautiful snow, down

---

from heaven to live with me, to keep me warm and safe.

I took the Dyson to the dump, it threatens me from the corner. It wants to suck you up and confine our love to a plastic cell. Don't worry, I wouldn't let that happen.

You'll never guess what I did! You'll feel better when I tell you this. Today I cut my toe nail off, and I put mine next to yours. I spooned them. Your big one around my little one: two half moons in the night.

I take it with me when I have to go out. I put it in my hand with a piece of sellotape over it to keep you safe. Sometimes when I almost forget it's there, I close my fist tight, by accident, and it pricks me. Lately, I've been more forgetful and now I have a sore patch right in my palm, and it hurts me all the time.

I don't forget *you*. I forget the toe nail.

I went up to the bathroom yesterday, and I put it back where I found it. I was worried you'd think I was being silly.

But then I went to bed and could not sleep. I couldn't bear to think of you alone on those cold, cold tiles. So I went and got you again and brought you in. I held you so tight. And when I woke up, you were broken into two.

And I knew you'd gone.

Have a wander round your home or garden, and choose something small enough for you to hold in one hand. Look at it for a while. Touch it, listen to it, smell it. If you can do so without poisoning yourself, taste it.

Where did it come from? How was it made? What of? How did it grow? What is it used for? How did it get into your space? What could happen to it, or what could it make happen? What predicaments might it cause, or resolve, symbolize or represent? In A. L. Kennedy's short story 'Wasps' (in her collection *What Becomes* (Vintage)), the eponymous stinging insects appear in inexplicable numbers in a house where a couple's marriage is falling apart. In Tim O'Brien's 'The Things They Carried', a soldier in a war zone wears his girlfriend's pantyhose round his neck for luck. In Helen Simpson's 'Lentils and Lilies' (in her collection *Hey Yeah Right Get a Life* (Vintage)), a baby sticks a lentil up its nose.

Put your small object on the desk in front of you, and stare at it for a while. When you are ready, build a small (500–600 words) story around it.

Longer short stories

Remember that list you compiled a few chapters ago, of short stories that you would like to have with you on a desert island? Have another look at it and see how many of the stories are more than 10,000 words long.

Not many, I would guess. Long short stories are not a particularly popular form.

Long short stories are hard work, for reader and writer alike. The reader of a long short story has to give it the same sort of attention as is demanded by a novel, but for less reward, at least in terms of reading time. The short story fan who hopes to see the world in a grain of sand doesn't necessarily want to end up scrutinizing a lump of rock.

As a writer of long short stories, you have to develop, hone and use the skills of a novelist. You also have to keep them in check. And to make matters worse, long short stories are difficult to sell.

With so much against them, you might wonder why long short stories ever get written at all.

The best reason – the only good reason – is that your content seems to demand it. Fay Weldon's 'Polaris' (in her collection *Polaris and Other Stories* (Coronet)), which is about 15,000 words long, tells a cluster of tales about the men who operate a nuclear-armed submarine, and about what their wives, lovers and pets get up to in their absence. The predicament is one of the biggest in the world – would these pleasant, ordinary-seeming guys really launch nuclear Armageddon if ordered to do so? The resolution is quiet in its optimism and bathos. Given its material, the story couldn't be any shorter.

I felt the same about my own 11,000-word story 'How Do You Pronounce Nulliparous?' (in my collection *How Do You Pronounce Nulliparous?* (Five Leaves)), which concerns a woman who has chosen not to have children, but is now reaching an age when it will soon cease to be a choice. It didn't feel like a big enough predicament for a novel, but it was too big, too multifaceted, too involved with the past and the future as well as the present, to make a really short story. So I wrote it as a long one.

Betty Burton's 'Women Are Bloody Marvellous' (in her collection *Women Are Bloody Marvellous* (Grafton)) is a series of letters that show the development of a relationship between a white British woman, who thinks of herself as a political liberal, and her black servant in South Africa in the 1980s. The actual events of the story could be summed up in a page or two, but the length (around 8,000 words) and the letters allow it to breathe.

The long short story has an honourable pedigree, including among its practitioners Dorothy Parker, Mavis Gallant and, of course, Anton Chekhov. Long short stories can satisfy, enchant, stimulate. So have a go at writing one. But beware: if your short story is going to be long, make sure it's because you chose to write it that way, not because you started writing and couldn't find a way to stop.

Insight

A long short story occupies uncomfortable territory between two more popular forms. If you want your reader to enter that territory with you, and stay there, invite them in hospitably, and make them comfortable.

TWO EXERCISES FOR WRITING LONG SHORT STORIES

- Think about two fictional people in a relationship that has lasted for at least ten years. It can be any kind of relationship – hairdresser and client, priest and penitent, technical support person and customer. Or they can be lovers, friends, family members.
- Identify the time and circumstances in which the relationship began.
- Identify the time and circumstances in which it ended – or, if it is still going on, the stage it is at now.
- Identify two high points and two low points in the intervening ten years.
- You now have six key moments in the story of this relationship: beginning, end (or current state), two high points and two low

points in between. Use each of these key moments as a high point of tension, suspense or danger (physical or emotional) within the longer story. The link between these moments is the ongoing relationship that you have chosen as the main theme of the story.

- Imagine a person with a flaw, an obsession, a need, a strength, a weakness, or a habit that has been a recurring theme in their life. Maybe they are always making lists, or stalking people, or falling hopelessly in love. Maybe they make frequent radical changes to their appearance (by dieting, by having cosmetic surgery, by shaving their head), or give things away, or build business empires, or can't hold a job for more than a week before getting sacked.
- Write a short episode showing how this character trait manifested itself in their early life. Then write an episode showing how it manifested itself in mid-life.
- Now write an episode showing how it manifests itself today.
- Has this person developed in relation to this aspect of their character? Is this development the story? Or have they remained static – exactly as they were when this characteristic first appeared? Is that the story? Write the story.

10 THINGS TO KEEP IN MIND

1 A short story can be as short or as long as you like ...

2 ... unless you are writing it for a particular market. Then write it to the length that market requires.

3 Even if there is no external constraint on the length of your story, set a length for yourself, and try to stick to it: it's a good discipline, and allows you to build up the skills needed for different lengths of story.

4 Read stories of different lengths.

5 Whatever its length or brevity, a short story should always feel complete. It should not read like a synopsis, a summary or an extract from something longer.

6 If you find you have to cut a story to make it fit a particular length, make up for it by adding intensity to the material you leave behind.

7 Flash fiction should be like a flash of light: a quick, startling experience for the reader.

8 Pay attention to jokes and anecdotes, whether you hear them from friends or professional performers. Which ones make you laugh – the short, sharp ones, or the long shaggy-dog stories? Note how they work, how they are structured and how they are told. Learn from them.

9 Resist the temptation to end your story with a moral or summing-up. It's a waste of words, and it should be unnecessary. (If you haven't made your point by the time you get to the end, a final nudge is not going to save your story.)

10 Long short stories are difficult to write successfully. So have a go.

8

Finding the plot

In this chapter, you will learn:
- *what is meant by a 'plot'*
- *elements of plot*
- *the pros and cons of plotting your short stories in advance.*

In my notebook I find several pages devoted to a man I overheard on a bus talking to a friend of his. Both men were strangers to me.

The main speaker had just got back from a holiday, and his eccentricity was that he listed in detail every meal that was served in the guest house where he had been staying.

He seemed to have perfect recall: I see from my notebook that on Monday for breakfast he had porridge and scrambled egg. Lunch was tomato soup and cold chicken and salad, with apple crumble to follow. Dinner was fish pie, and cheese and biscuits. Tuesday's breakfast was boiled eggs. Lunch was macaroni cheese. And so on, and on and on and on.

His friend did not ask 'Why are you telling me this?' – for all I knew, this might have been the speaker's normal style of discourse. Or perhaps he was doing it as a bet. But as an outsider, I couldn't see where the monologue (I won't flatter it by calling it a conversation) was going. It seemed to me that the speaker had lost the plot. Or perhaps he never had one in the first place.

Insight

The expression 'losing the plot' has come to mean being in a state of uncongenial confusion or disorientation, of not knowing what is going on. That's not what the reader of your short stories wants, or what you want for

The man on the bus's list of menus was not a plot, but he could have turned it into one. He could have introduced an element of the unexpected by breaking into his list of unremarkable English boarding house food, with the announcement that on Thursday morning he came down to breakfast and was presented with a plate of boiled seaweed. That would have demanded a plot because I (and, I suspect, his friend and everyone else on the bus) would have wanted to know why. Had what sounded like the most conventional of caterers taken leave of their senses? Had someone watched one cookery programme too many? Had the proprietor of the guest house run out of money and been forced to improvise? Any or all of those could have been developed into a plot.

Similarly, if the speaker had said 'On Friday I was rushed to hospital with food poisoning', that too would have been a plot, as it would have contained an element of cause and effect. It would have given a context for his gastronomic reminiscences by showing what all that food led to. The same would have applied if he had ended the conversation by standing up to leave the bus, saying to his friend, 'Well, it's been nice talking to you, but I'm off to Weight Watchers.'

Insight

A plot has to be more than an account of what occurred. If such an account causes the reader to ask 'so what?', then it is not a plot.

When to plot

Sometimes a plot will come to you fully formed.

It might be something that happened to you: a complete incident with a beginning, a middle and an end. You were walking through the city centre when you recognized someone you used to be at primary school with. All you can remember about them is that once when they visited your house you caught them rifling with a knife in your piggy bank. But that was a lifetime ago – children do things like that, and they don't mean any harm by it. You stop, suggest a coffee and have a pleasant chat about the old days. It's only later that you discover your wallet is missing.

Life is not always so tidy (albeit expensively so), but it is sometimes, and, when it is, it saves the short story writer a lot of work. Be grateful (even if you have lost your wallet) and write it down.

Insight
If a plot comes to you fully formed, grab it with both hands. The rest of the time, you have to work at it.

Your story may be a new take on one that already exists – a myth or legend or fairy tale. Once again, much of the plotting will already have been done for you.

More usually, a story begins as a sort of mental itch, an obsession or preoccupation. It may be something you dreamed or heard through gossip or on the news. It may be a task set by someone else – a themed competition, or an assignment concocted by your writing group. Such a stimulus may be a brilliant way to start you off, but it won't lead you to a satisfying short story unless you give some thought to constructing or finding a plot. What are the elements of a good plot?

Elements of plotting

PREDICAMENT AND RESOLUTION

This basic plot structure has already been discussed in Chapter 3. Plot your story by putting someone in a predicament – that is, a situation of difficulty, danger, uncertainty, embarrassment or unfulfilled desire. Show how they got there, and show them trying to get out. Have something unexpected but uncontrived happen that either assists them, or obstructs them further. Have them resolve matters, or fail to do so. It's not the only plot, but it's a standard, a classic, one to fall back on.

CAUSE AND EFFECT

As E. M. Forster famously pointed out in his book *Aspects of the Novel*, 'the king died and then the queen died' is not a plot. It is a brief account of two events which may or may not be connected. It only becomes a plot when you introduce an element of cause and effect: 'The king died and then the queen died of grief.'

Here's another example:

> *My husband left me. My cat died.*

That is not a plot, but it can easily be turned into one, by introducing an element of cause and effect:

> *My husband left me. My cat died, flattened by my husband's car as he sped down the drive in his eagerness to get away from me and into the arms of his boyfriend.*

Sometimes the effect is on the narrator:

> *My husband left me. My cat died. This has been the worst week of my life.*

> *My husband left me. My cat died. This has been the best week of my life.*

Spend some time looking for elements of cause and effect in the short stories you read. In V.S. Pritchett's 'The Saint' (in *The Penguin Book of International Short Stories*), a ridiculous incident involving a punt and a preacher causes the narrator to lose his religious faith. In Elizabeth Taylor's 'Flesh' (in her collection *The Devastating Boys* (Virago)), an elderly couple try, as part of their holiday romance, to have sex. Their mutual desire is strong, but their bodily infirmities cause failure and sadness.

Look for cause and effect, too, in myths and legends, and in the oft-told tales that come up in conversation, recur in different forms on the news, or keep the storylines going in soap operas.

CHARACTERS

These are the people in your stories – the people who do things, and to whom things are done. The people who come under pressure. The people whose conflicts – with each other, with outsiders and strangers, with the forces of fate and nature, with the wider world – generate your short stories. These are so important that they have a chapter of their own in this book. See Chapter 10.

UNEXPECTEDNESS

Surprises and coincidences can energize your stories, but they need to happen early. They should open things up, not close them down. If your story is about someone with money problems, having him or her solve them on the last page by winning the lottery is unlikely to be convincing or satisfying. We all know 'it could be you', but the truth is that it probably won't be.

On the other hand, a story that *begins* with an unexpected acquisition of wealth by a person who, up until now, was up to their ears in debt, has huge possibilities. The money may transform their life for the better, or they may squander it on riotous living and end up back where they started. Or they may fall victim to unscrupulous relatives or identity fraudsters, and watch helplessly as the money leaks away.

If you insist on introducing an element of the unexpected late in your story, you should at least foreshadow it, so that the reader, at the same time as being surprised, can realize that they saw it coming (or could have, if they had been paying closer attention). If it's a whodunnit and the guilty party is the person you would be least likely to suspect, let that person act suspiciously long before there is any suspicion of him. Then when the reader learns the truth, they can think, 'Ah yes, I should have noticed that…' If someone confesses out of the blue that they are in love with the main character, this will be a more satisfying outcome if we can look back on their behaviour earlier in the story and identify the symptoms of early unrequited love.

Insight

It's fine to begin your story with a coincidence, but risky to end with one.

QUESTIONS AND ANSWERS

At the beginning of the story, the reader should have a question. It might be: 'Who is this person?' or 'How did he get into this mess, and how is he going to get out of it?' It might be: 'Will the path of true love run smooth?' or 'Is it really true love?' Or it might be: 'Who is telling us this story, and why?' The plot of the story should provide answers to at least some of these questions, not all at once, but at a pace that will sustain the reader's interest. Sometimes the answer will be that there is no answer.

BEGINNINGS, MIDDLES AND ENDS

This is a traditional approach, and, like many traditional things, it sometimes gets dismissed as old-fashioned. But, like the little black dress, it has survived the test of time and is a safe choice for a newcomer to short story writing. The beginning should establish the situation, the normal life and background of the character, the once-upon-a-time element. The middle should disrupt this. The ending should restore some order. This does not have to be 'they all lived happily ever after' – it might, on the contrary, be the stillness of death or loss or other tragedy. But there should be a sense of resumption, of restoration, a pleasing contrast between things being almost as they were, and someone or something having moved on.

Here's an example of how it might work, using that old nursery classic about Goldilocks and the Three Bears:

BEGINNING: A family of bears lived a life of contented domesticity in a house in the forest. One morning they went for a pre-breakfast walk, leaving the door unlocked.

MIDDLE: A little girl called Goldilocks, who happened to be passing, entered the house, sampled the bears' breakfast, and fell asleep in one of their beds. The bears returned and found evidence of an intruder. Unnerved and angry, they prowled around, looking for the culprit, getting closer and closer to the place where Goldilocks lay, asleep, unaware and unprotected.

END: The bears discovered Goldilocks. She woke up to the terrifying spectacle of three bears looking down at her. She screamed and ran away, leaving the bears to enjoy what remained of their breakfast.

That's all very well for Goldilocks, you may be thinking, but it wouldn't work for you: your stories don't always fall so neatly into beginnings, middles and ends, and you're not even sure you want them to.

It's a fair point, and it raises the question of whether it is always a good idea to plot a short story in advance. There's no one answer to this: it depends on what kind of writer you are, and what kind of story you are writing. And it's not either/or: even if you decide to plot a story in detail before finalizing it, your strategy for doing that may simply be to write early drafts and wait for the elements of plot to emerge.

Insight

A well-constructed plot is like the foundations of a building: you can't see it, but, if it wasn't there, the entire edifice would be in danger of collapse.

To plan or not to plan?

What are the pros and cons of plotting your story in advance?

PROS

▶ If you are writing an assignment (whether it's for your writing group, a competition, for an editor or for yourself), with a specific subject, word-length and delivery deadline, you need a strategy to achieve these. A carefully worked-out plot, and writing schedule, ensures that you do not wander away from the main point, exceed the word-length or run out of time. For example, if you have undertaken to deliver, by Friday, a story about a hostage, you might decide that on Monday you will write about the hostage being taken, and on Tuesday you will describe the conditions of their captivity. On Wednesday you will describe a failed rescue attempt, on Thursday you will get them out of there. On Friday, just when they thought they were free, you will have them recaptured.
▶ If you know in advance what is going to happen, it is easier to keep your story tight, focused and short.
▶ Tight plotting adds to the intensity of a story, and reduces the risk of distracting your reader with mistakes or inconsistencies, such as letting your character know things that they could not know, or allowing them to be in two places at once.

▶ You may feel that your stories are too complex and subtle to be distilled down to a simple formula. Knowing that your life is not a series of neat beginnings, middles and ends, you may see no reason to impose them on the lives of the characters in your stories. You may prefer to write stories that evoke the randomness, irrationality and inconclusiveness of real life as you perceive it. Go ahead – but remember you've got a reader out there, someone who picked up your story because a story was what they wanted to read. So shake off the shackles of plotting if you must, but try still to give your reader a tale in which something happens, something they have reason to care about.

▶ You may be the sort of writer who simply doesn't know what is going to happen in your story until you start writing. It is the act of writing that stimulates your creativity, rather than vice versa. Planning in advance doesn't work for you; you just have to start writing and wait for the plot to emerge.

▶ Plotting in advance can be constraining rather than supportive: it may block out ideas that you might have preferred to use. It makes it more difficult to think on the page.

▶ You might feel that if you can do justice to your story in a plot outline or synopsis, there's not much point in writing it to a greater length.

These are all fair points, even if they do sometimes appear to contradict each other. One way of resolving the contradictions is to think less in terms of plots and stories, and more in terms of shapes and structures. These are the subject of the next chapter.

10 THINGS TO KEEP IN MIND

1 Your readers want to be told a short story. So tell them one. Make something happen.

2 Make the readers care what happens next. Plant questions in their minds, and make them wait for the answers.

3 A plot is more than a sequence of events. It is also about the connections between them.

4 The very fact that the story is being told by a particular person, in a particular way, may be part of the plot.

5 Sometimes you will want to plot your story in advance; on other occasions you may prefer to draft on the page and wait for connected events and unanswered questions to emerge. Neither approach is better or worse than the other. Try both.

6 Look out for ready-made plots in the world around you – connected sequences of events that you experience or hear about, and find satisfying. Put them in your notebook, and learn from them.

7 Be on the lookout, too, for unconnected events, and find ways to connect them.

8 It's fine to use surprise or coincidence to set up a predicament, but, unless you are in the realms of fantasy or magical realism (see Chapter 14), not to resolve it. If you insist on ending a story on a surprise or a coincidence, find a way to foreshadow it.

9 Make sure your reader always has something to hope for and something to worry about.

10 If you don't feel you can plot your story in advance – either on this particular occasion, or ever – read the next chapter, and see if structures will help.

Short story structures

In this chapter, you will learn:
• *ways of structuring your short stories.*

'Writing a short story is a high-wire act, sentence by sentence, foot by foot,' writes author Alison MacLeod. 'Very few story writers work with the safety net of a plot conceived in advance' ('Alison MacLeod's Top 10 Short Stories', *The Guardian*, 23 October 2007). Whether or not you are one of those few, there will be times when the safety net is unavailable. You don't have a plot. You don't know what is going to happen in your story – one of your purposes in writing it is to find out.

In these circumstances – staying with MacLeod's tightrope-walking metaphor – you can sometimes rely instead on the balancing pole of structure to create your story and keep it going. Think less in terms of *what* is going to happen in your story, and more in terms of *how* those happenings (once you have decided or discovered what they are) are going to be shaped.

Narrative arc

Make a mental image of your story as a line which curves upwards every time you give your characters (and therefore your reader) something to worry about. The curve goes back down again as the tension is eased. The winding-up and winding-down can either be tortuously slow and suspense-filled, or shockingly abrupt.

Insight
Make sure your reader always has something to hope for and something to worry about.

To imagine such an arc, think of a person who is currently safe but who is about to encounter danger. One example might be a woman getting off a bus at night and walking the short distance to her home. She is calm and cheerful; there is nothing to worry about. The line is flat.

When she becomes aware of a man's footsteps following her and getting closer, her tension rises, and so does the reader's: the line of the arc curves upwards. It reaches its highest point when the man pounces, puts his hand over her mouth and tries to snatch her handbag. But, trained as she is in unarmed combat, she sees him off with a couple of well-aimed blows. He lies groaning on the ground as she hurries into her house, locks the door and calls the police. Justice has been done, good order has been restored: the villain has been punished, his intended victim is safe. The line of the narrative is flat once more.

A story can contain several arcs. In Maeve Binchy's 'Murmurs in Montrose' (see Chapter 4), Gerry is coming out of a nursing home after treatment for alcoholism. Supposedly cured, his challenge now is to resume his old life, rebuilding his personal and professional relationships without going back to the bottle. He passes through various moments of temptation, each of which constitutes a single narrative arc. There is a build-up of anxiety for him, for his loved ones, for us as readers — will he drink or won't he? If he does, what then? The story is structured round a sequence of linked episodes, a continuous line of arcs. Each episode has different content but the same structure. The overall arc concerns a man struggling with an addiction, and his loved ones and not-so-loved ones struggling with him.

Predicament/resolution (but with camouflage)

We have seen how a simple story can be structured by putting someone into a predicament and waiting to see how (and if) this will be resolved. The trouble with this approach is that lots of people know about it. They can see it coming.

So camouflage it. Make it look like something else. Suppose you want to write a short story about John and Mary on their wedding day. It is told from the point of view of John, whose predicament is that he would prefer to remain single. At a crucial moment in the ceremony, he catches sight of a flake of nail polish peeling from Mary's thumbnail.

It annoys him – couldn't she be bothered to have a proper manicure, today of all days? He realizes that, although he sort of loves her, he doesn't really like her very much, and he certainly doesn't want to live the rest of his life with her sloppy personal habits. He flees.

A plot involving a runaway bridegroom or bride has to be dramatic. But if you are committed to it before you start writing, you may give the game away before you are ready. If, on the other hand, you use something else to shape your story – another structure – you can camouflage your real intentions, allowing the reader to enjoy looking at one thing while your real plot is creeping quietly up a side-aisle like a displaced suitor, leading to an ending that is both surprising and inevitable – the perfect combination.

Insight
Use events and procedures with which your reader is already familiar – ceremonies and social rituals, security procedures at airports, childbirth, court trials, cooking a complex dish, major news events – to give structure to your stories, and to cover up the bare bones of your plot.

A wedding is always a story, with a high point of symbolic drama, when, after months or perhaps years of preparation, two single people change their status and enter into a (theoretically at least) unbreakable commitment. Whether it is a huge do in a cathedral or a brief visit to the town hall, you can cut at the key moment from the grandeur of the building and the ceremony, to that tiny peeling flake of nail varnish – or other detail – that allows someone to realize that they are doing the wrong thing, and gives them the courage or cowardice to flee.

But get it right. If you are not sure of every detail of the ceremony that your couple would be having, research it. Is it a civil ceremony, or religious? What religion? What exactly does everyone say, do, wear? You won't use every detail that your research uncovers, but the knowledge you acquire will enable you to write with confidence. The details you do use will add conviction.

Try this
Choose a large public event that you have witnessed, either in person or on TV. (A sporting event? The 9/11 attack on the Twin Towers? A natural disaster?) Research it to refresh your memory and to get the details right. Use this event as background and structure for a story about someone losing a precious object.

Circles

A circle can give tightness to a story, without too much restriction. Your character ends up more or less where they started.

> **Try this**
> **Write the first sentence of your story** – something like this perhaps:
>
> *It was 3 a.m. and the baby was crying.*
>
> **Then write the last sentence,** which should be similar to the first, but not exactly the same: it should show some development, either in the predicament itself, or the character's response to it, or maybe just the passage of time:
>
> *It was 4 a.m. and the baby was still crying.*
>
> **Now write the bit in between.** It may be an account of the methods – some sensible and kind, some less so – used by the character to pacify the baby. It may be a development in the character's reflections on the pains and joys of parenthood.
>
> Or it may have nothing to do with parenthood – the person hearing the baby may be the next-door neighbour. The baby's crying may just be background noise to an entirely different story, a story which, nevertheless, has a baby's cries as its beginning and its end.

A journey

In a journey from one place to another, you have a ready-made structure for a short story. Whether your character is strolling down the road to buy milk, or kayaking alone across the Atlantic, they have a beginning (setting out), a middle (the trip) and an end (arrival, or failure to arrive). There is scope for surprise, causality, predicament, resolution, suspense, and questions with delayed answers. A physical journey can also give structure to a metaphorical journey: what is happening in your character's inner world as he or she moves from one location to another?

> **Try this**
> **Think of five real journeys** and write each of them on a separate piece of paper. A single phrase is enough – 'from London to New York'

for example, or 'from home to school' or 'from prison cell to execution chamber'. Put the pieces of paper in a pile.

Then do the same **with five abstract or metaphorical journeys:** 'from rags to riches', 'from belief to cynicism', 'from love to hate' (or vice versa).

Pick one at random from each pile, match them, and write the story. You could write for example about a person on their way to their execution, travelling in their mind between hate and love. Or you could write about someone on a flight between London and New York, discovering that their erstwhile riches are now rags. Whatever journey you choose, let the outward trappings of the physical journey interact with and symbolize the inner one.

Insight

If you are structuring your story around a journey, and if it is practical for you to do so, make that journey yourself. Write notes at every stage about what your fictional character would see, hear, smell, taste, feel, hope for and worry about, and what these would say about the inner journey that the character is making at the same time.

If you can't make the journey yourself, research it. Interview someone who has made that journey. Read books about it. If the sort of vehicle they travel in is no longer around, try and find a museum that has one in display. Go and look at it for a while. Identify small details, be open to unexpected insights. Imagine how it would feel to go somewhere in that vehicle. Let the movement give structure and energy to your story.

Pictures

Imagine you are commissioning an artist or photographer to illustrate three key moments of your story. Write the brief that you would give, describing the sorts of images and visual clues and cues you would hope to see in the illustrations. Make these moments the high points of your plot: build the rest of the story around them.

Ripples

A small event disturbs our perception of a character about whom we thought we knew all there was to know. A sadistic bully performs an act of genuine kindness; a hitherto-devoted husband or wife is successfully seduced into infidelity; a jockey starving himself in order to reach the required body weight for an important race is seen to eat six Mars bars.

Let the repercussions of these small events ripple outwards into a plot.

Sometimes the ripples disturb a whole community: Sylvia Plath's 'Mothers' (in her collection *Johnny Panic and the Bible of Dreams* (Faber)) starts as a low-key, good-natured, fish-out-of-water tale of a young American housewife living in England in the late 1950s, and paying her first visit to a mothers' group based around the local church. All seems benign – until, almost as an aside, it is revealed that it is not the American visitor who is the fish out of water but one of her neighbours, who is – scandalously, in a rural English village before the dawn of more permissive times – divorced. It's a tiny episode, but the ripples extend forward into the social changes that lie in wait, for this community, for everyone.

Lists

You can structure your story around lists. Fay Weldon's 'Christmas Lists' (in her collection *Polaris and Other Stories* (Coronet)) tells the story of a marriage, from happy, penniless student courtship, through Thatcherite prosperity, to late middle-aged bankruptcy. It's a long, somewhat rambling story, held together by the lists the wife makes at Christmas.

'Home Helper' by Amanda Gersh (in *Dinaane: Short Stories by South African Women*, edited by Maggie Davey (Telegram Books)) is a coming-of-age story about a young girl who joins the Brownies and yearns for the badges that she will one day be able to stitch onto her sleeve as marks of Brownie achievement. Each badge marks a section of the story.

The hero's adventure

No discussion of story structure is complete without a reference to *The Hero with a Thousand Faces* by Joseph Campbell. First published in 1949, this book identified recurrent themes and structures in the myths and stories of cultures ancient and modern, from all over the world. It suggested, in the words of script consultant and screenwriting teacher Christopher Vogler, that 'they are all basically the same story – retold endlessly in infinite variation' (Christopher Vogler, 'A Practical Guide to *The Hero with a Thousand Faces*' (available online)).

The essentials of the story have been used to structure the adventures of fictional heroes from Odysseus to Beowulf, from King Arthur to Oliver Twist, from Holden Caulfield to Lisbeth Salander – not to mention the Famous Five, the Secret Seven and the children in *The Lion, the Witch and the Wardrobe*. They are and can be reused by contemporary writers, including you.

Vogler's article is a guide to mythic structures and ways in which you might use them in your own storytelling. This is not a recipe for 'formula fiction' – as Vogler stresses, 'The myth is infinitely flexible, capable of endless variation without sacrificing any of its magic.'

Here is one approach to structuring a story around a hero's adventure:

- Your main character is going about his or her daily life when something out-of-the-ordinary happens.
- The extraordinary event brings with it a challenge, a call to adventure – which the hero initially resists.
- Under pressure of circumstances, the hero gives in and sets off on the adventure, encountering dangers, uncertainties, helpers and obstacles on the way. In myth, fantasy or fairy tale, these might include encounters with witches and wizards (benign or

otherwise), and quests for magic stones, swords and substances. In a more realistic setting, the encounters might be with difficult bosses, mobsters, lovers/seducers, kindly old teachers or long-lost parents; the quest may be for love, or money, or to overthrow a tyrant, thwart and/or catch a villain, or save the world. The hero is put through ordeals and tests, and subjected to rules. Breaking the rules adds to the hero's isolation.

- The story may end in a number of ways: the hero finds what he or she was looking for, and returns home, wiser and enriched; or fails to do so, and despairs; or, failing to do so, makes peace with that. Or the quest may continue.

You can probably think of a great many films, plays, novels, ancient legends and even real-life stories which fit this structure. You may have made a hero's journey of your own, or currently be embarked upon one. It is all around us, and, in the words of Christopher Vogler, 'It will outlive us all.'

It is less commonly used in short stories, precisely because short stories are short and the hero's adventure is usually long. If you tried to cram all the material into one short story, even a long short story, you would probably end up with a novel-in-synopsis, which is the worst of all worlds. Choose a single episode of your hero's adventure, and write it with intensity: for example the moment when he or she overcomes reluctance and decides to face the challenge, or one of the encounters with wise or evil strangers. Let the rest of the ancient mythic structure glitter and shift in the background.

The end

Whatever structure you use for your stories, keep in mind that the ending should be credible and satisfying.

- ▶ If you started with a predicament, end with a resolution. If you envisaged your story as a circle, move towards an ending that is as close as possible to the beginning.
- ▶ If you have started a ripple on a smooth surface, leave it rippling.
- ▶ If it is a list story, end with the last item on the list. Or – as in 'Christmas Lists' by Fay Weldon – a decision to make no more lists.

- ▶ If it is a journey, end on the moment of arrival, or failure to arrive.
- ▶ If you end on a twist, a shock or a coincidence, make sure it has been foreshadowed, however subtly.

Insight

Even if the action that ends the story is a surprise, it should be in keeping with what the reader knows about the person who performs it.

The pace of the story should pick up towards the end. However much the reader has been enjoying your writing, once she knows she is near the end, she is like a horse scenting home. Let her get there. Don't explain. If an explanation is needed, it should have come before. Zoë Heller, judge of the 2010 Bridport Prize for short stories, reported that 'Many good stories failed at the final hurdle... by spelling out, with leaden seriousness, the "significance" of what had gone before' (*The Bridport Prize 2010* (Redcliffe Press)). You have been warned!

Insight

In short story writing, as in life, be ready to quit while you're ahead. Don't feel you have to spell everything out. Suppose your hero is trapped under a collapsed building, following an earthquake, with sewage rising around her from a burst pipe, and rats running over her face. If that is the end of her story, end there. You don't need to describe every detail of her eventual demise. If you've built up the horror with sufficient skill and intensity, the reader will imagine that. The horror your reader feels at your hero's plight is a measure of the strength of your writing. It means that you are ahead. So quit. End. Leave them there. It feels brutal. It is brutal. It's a short story.

10 THINGS TO KEEP IN MIND

1 When you've got a story to tell but are not sure how to tell it, try to envisage it as a shape or a structure – an arc, a circle, ripples, a journey.

2 Look for shapes and structures in the stories that you read.

3 Let structures hold your stories together, but don't let them be too obvious to the reader. Camouflage them.

4 Factual material can give solidity to your stories – provided it is relevant and accurate.

5 Read folk tales, legends and traditional myths, from other cultures as well as your own. Note recurrent themes and archetypal characters, and adapt them for your stories.

6 Use mythic structures, but don't let them use you. If you borrow characters from myth, make sure that, in the context of your story, they are interesting individuals, and of their time and place. Don't feel you have to cram huge amounts of material into your short story just because the original myth demands it. Look for small episodes within the hero's adventure, and make your story out of them. Let the mythic structures shift and twinkle in the background.

7 Speed up the pace of your story as you get close to the end.

8 If you end your story on a surprise, don't let it be too contrived or incongruous. As well as surprising, it should feel inevitable.

9 Don't end your story with an explanation or a moral. If explanations and morals are important, they should be intrinsic to the story, not tagged on at the end.

10 However you make your stories – plotting them, structuring them or a bit of each – make sure that at all times your reader has something to hope for, and something to worry about. And you as author are entitled to the same. If you find you have stopped hoping for things for your characters, or stopped worrying about them, it may mean that you have lost the thread of your story. Go back to the point where you last cared, really cared, about what happened, and start again from there.

10

The people in your stories

In this chapter, you will learn:
- *how to create fictional characters*
- *how to make them come to life on the pages of your short stories*
- *how to make your readers care about what happens to them.*

Short stories are about people – the things people do, the things that are done to them, the ways people change.

(Short stories can also be about animals or even inanimate objects – stories intended for children frequently are, as are stories in the magical realist genre. See Chapter 14. But the animals and inanimate objects have to display some human-like qualities – thinking, choosing, reflecting, having relationships, using language – if they are to engage the reader's interest.)

Most of the people in short stories do not exist and never have existed. Even when they are based on real people, the author will probably have changed them for the purpose of the story. Why, then, should the reader care about them?

Some people don't care. Helene Hanff, author of *84 Charing Cross Road*, wrote, 'I never can get interested in things that didn't happen to people who never lived.' Put that way, it is a view that is hard to argue with. But the continued existence and popularity of written fiction, not to mention fictional films, and radio and TV programmes, shows that many people can and do 'get interested'. Even Helene Hanff changed her mind when she discovered Jane Austen and 'went out of my mind for *Pride and Prejudice*'. Hanff did not reveal what it was about this particular book that led her to reconsider, but I think we can hazard a guess that Elizabeth Bennet and Mr Darcy might have had something to do with it.

Characters, in other words. Imaginary people who are so strongly portrayed that the reader believes in them, not in the sense of expecting them to turn up on the doorstep, but in the sense of recognizing them, laughing at them and with them, fearing for them, being annoyed by them, quoting their sayings, learning from their wisdom and folly, returning to the story again and again for the pleasure of remaking their acquaintance.

How can the newcomer to short story writing create powerful, memorable, involving characters?

One character at a time

At first, confine yourself to one or two main characters per story.

If as a beginner you try to manage more, you may make your reader feel that they have arrived at a party full of strangers, given by a host whose idea of introducing guests is to reel off a list of names, relationships and/or job titles: 'this is my cousin Dennis, he's a gardener; Bill lives next door and works at the Foreign Office; this is Jackie, she's staying with us for a while.' In those circumstances it is unlikely that the guest will remember anyone, let alone care what happens to them.

But if the host introduces the guest to just one person and leaves them to converse, they may discover things about each other that are interesting or at least unexpected: Dennis has planted cannabis in the host's rockery, Bill has just got back from Afghanistan, Jackie is homeless. This is the sort of information that turns a stranger into an individual, which is what you need to do when creating fictional characters.

Show, don't tell

We have already explored this principle as a way of adding to the intensity of descriptions of places and things. The same applies when introducing characters.

Telling is the approach whereby the narrator gives an opinion on a character, or makes a value judgement, without giving any reason for it. **Showing** means giving the reader information which will lead him or her to understand, and perhaps share, the narrator's view.

If a first-person narrative begins with the words 'my boss is a bully', it is not actually telling you anything about the narrator's boss. It is telling you something about the narrator – i.e. that she dislikes and feels intimidated by the person she works for. Whether or not this is justified remains to be revealed. For all we know at this stage in the story, the boss may be a mild-mannered individual who wouldn't hurt a fly, except when provoked beyond endurance by the sloppy work and insolent manner (and endless complaining) of our narrator. If the narrator wants to get you on her side – if the author of the story wants to get you on the narrator's side – they will have to *show* the boss being a bully:

▶ My head of department conducts spot checks on his staff's packed lunches, and makes us throw out anything that he considers unhealthy.

▶ The Managing Director's secretary has just emailed to say that Wages & Salaries will be deducting £35 from my wages for the cost of private phone calls from work – calls I never made.

▶ My boss keeps a replica gun in her desk. She's pointing it at me now.

These are statements of fact (albeit in the context of a fictional story), rather than just impressions, or moans. Any one of them would make a livelier beginning to a short story than the unsubstantiated 'my boss is a bully'. By showing a specific incident, it shows character. It makes something happen. It opens the way for something else to happen. It invites the reader to take sides, to think 'I once had a boss like that' (or even 'That's a good idea, maybe I should try it on my staff').

Try this

Turn the following examples of telling, into showing. Reveal what the character is like by showing them in action:

▶ The headmaster was in a bad mood.
▶ You could see that the checkout assistant's mind was not on the job.
▶ My baby is so funny.
▶ The chef's personal habits left a lot to be desired.

Get physical

When introducing a character, how much physical description should you give?

It depends on two things: how important the person's looks are to the story, and who is describing whom.

In Chapter 4, we looked at point of view, and saw the different ways in which a room could be described, depending on what the connection is between the room and the describer. The same applies to characters. What is perceived will depend on who is doing the perceiving.

Try this

Think of an ordinary, pleasant-looking female teenager walking down the street. Write three separate paragraphs describing her from the point of view of:

1 her best friend
2 her mother
3 a sex pest who preys on teenage girls.

Ask yourself: which specific aspects of her appearance would each of these watchers notice and focus on?

In Raymond Carver's short story 'Fat' (in *The Penguin Book of International Short Stories, 1945–1985*, edited by Daniel Halpern), the fatness of the customer in the restaurant is what the story is about. The narrator, a very thin waitress, refers to it again and again, always noting specific details in ways that say as much about her, the observer, as they do about the fat man himself.

He is 'the fattest person I have ever seen', but he is 'neat-appearing and well-dressed enough'. That slightly grudging 'enough' gives an insight into the waitress's values, as does her appreciation of the man's polite conversation and good manners. When her co-workers refer to him as 'tub of guts' and 'really a fatty', she feels hurt on his behalf. She notes that he takes his jacket off to eat, that he breathes heavily, consumes large quantities of bread and butter between courses, and refers to himself as 'we'. She is fascinated and aroused by the sight of his 'long, thick, creamy fingers'. With this sort of approach – where the perceptions of the narrator are as important as the person being described – the reader gets two characters for the price of one.

••

Insight

If you are describing a character through another person's point of view, remember that what the observer perceives will be shaped by their relationship with, and attitude to, the character.

••

The physical description of the character can be drip-fed throughout the story, or you might choose to start with a thumbnail sketch or a telling metaphor, a joke or an image. In 'Witching Hour' (in *Tales of the Decongested*, vol. 1, edited by Rebekah Lattin-Rawstrone and Paul Blaney (Apis Books)), Sally Hinchcliffe describes Harold, the chairman of the town council, as 'the sort of man who could get from nought to incandescent in sixty seconds'. With his 'plumpening cheeks and shinily emerging scalp', he looks like 'a cross baby'. In Dorothy Parker's 'The Bolt behind the Blue' (in *The Collected Dorothy Parker* (Penguin)), Alicia Hazelton is the woman who has everything – or, as the author puts it, 'Fortune had upended her cornucopia to hurtle gifts upon Alicia Hazelton.'

On the more sinister side, in the title story of Angela Carter's collection *The Bloody Chamber* (Vintage Classics), the young, vulnerable bride describes the 'dark, leonine shape' of the head of her much-older husband, the 'streaks of pure silver in his dark mane' and his 'strange, heavy, almost waxen face'. And in the opening paragraph of Franz Kafka's 'In the Penal Settlement' (in the collection *Metamorphosis and Other Stories* (Penguin)), a man condemned to death is described as looking 'so like a submissive dog that one might have thought he could be left to run free on the surrounding hills and would only need to be whistled for when the execution was due to begin.'

> **Try this**
> Angela Carter's narrator compares her husband with a lion ('Leonine...' 'his dark mane'). Kafka compares the prisoner with a 'submissive dog'.
>
> Choose from your life or your imagination a person who in some ways resembles an animal. Use that resemblance to describe the person in two sentences.

Give your characters things to do

When you create a character, don't just describe them and leave them standing there; put them into action, give them something to do, something in addition to whatever earned them a role in your story in the first place.

Insight
Your characters should have a life off the page, as well as on it.

Their role in your story may be as a lover, a parent, a patient, a spy. But that's not all they are. Show them living their everyday life: working, gardening, claiming benefits, watching their investments grow, shoplifting, eating, relaxing, shopping, fighting, making love, trying to get to sleep. Let some of the events of the story happen while they are busy with something else. And let the other things that they are busy with precipitate the events of the story.

Use yourself as a character

You will probably write about yourself anyway, whether you intend to or not. But it won't always be in the way that a certain kind of reader expects. If you are, for example, a 30-something ornithologist, it won't necessarily be the 30-something ornithologist in your story who is most like you. You'll use your knowledge of ornithology to make this character convincing, but your inner thoughts and perceptions will probably be in another character entirely.

If you have a story to tell that is true and about you and you don't care who knows it, then go ahead and write it as an autobiographical short story. But don't imagine that the fact that it is true excuses you from the same obligations to make your story as interesting and accessible to your reader as if it was fiction. Above all, don't go in for lengthy bouts of self-analysis: the short story is not the place for this. If you want the world to know what you are like, or were like on the one particular occasion in which your story has its origins, don't tell; show yourself in action.

Allow for change and development

In stories, as in life, a character who never changes is uninteresting. So let your characters change.

Have them struggle to change; make something happen that forces them to change. Put them under pressure. For example, they might:

▶ lose all their money
▶ get kidnapped
▶ fall hopelessly in love
▶ lose their memory
▶ witness a crime and have to go into hiding.

Insight

First, create your character.

Then put him or her under pressure.

The person who is always on top of the world, but then falls, engages our sympathy – and perhaps our smugness, our *schadenfreude*. That's a story. The person who is always in debt, or unlucky in love, or drowning in domestic chaos, may wear out our patience and interest until the day when they suddenly have a wonderful new boy/girlfriend, plenty of money or a neat and gleaming home. That may be the beginning of the story, the middle or the end – but, without change, there is no story. (In the end, they may go back to their old ways – but it is still a story.)

> **Try this**
> Write a brief passage – ten lines maximum – about a character waking up one morning and going through their ordinary morning routine. By showing what that routine consists of, show something of what kind of person they are. (Anxious? Selfish? Greedy? Lazy? Kind? Obsessive?)
>
> Now interrupt the routine with an unexpected event.
>
> Put the character under pressure, and show how they deal with it.

Use contradictions and contrasts

Human beings are not always consistent. Look for contradictions in your characters. If someone is tough, show them being vulnerable. Give a cruel person a moment of kindness. And vice versa. Let the model husband or wife kick over the traces, if only in their imagination.

Avoid stereotypes

This isn't the place for a detailed discussion on which uses of language are offensive to some people, and whether they should, for that reason, be avoided or even banned. You will have your own views on where the dividing line comes between, on the one hand, fairness and sensitivity, and, on the other, what is sometimes referred to as 'political correctness gone mad' (usually by people who didn't support it even before it went mad).

Whatever your thoughts on this, there is one overwhelming reason why stereotypes – i.e. oversimplifications based on the idea that all people in a particular group or category are the same – should be avoided. *Stereotyping is bad writing.* It's lazy. It sends out a signal that you can't be bothered to think beyond the cliché.

If you want to write about a boring accountant, go ahead, but don't skimp on the characterization just because 'everyone knows' that accountants are boring. Quite apart from being a grave insult to the many fascinating and witty accountants out there, it makes for dull writing if you shrug off your responsibility to make your characters individual. The same applies if you want to write about a member of a particular ethnic group having an attitude to sex or work or religion that in some circles is thought to be 'typical' of that group. Go ahead and write it: but if your story is going to work, you have to make their actions convincing in terms of that individual in that situation.

Let them talk

The use of dialogue brings together many of the subjects already covered by this book – point of view, character, showing rather than telling, and, above all, keeping things brief and fast-moving. People reveal a huge amount about themselves through talking – not just what they say, but how they say it. Writing good dialogue is an important skill for the writer of short stories – so much so that it gets a chapter of its own, the next one.

10 THINGS TO KEEP IN MIND

1 Stories are about people. Readers are people. Your aim is to bring them together.

2 Don't tell your reader what your characters are like: show what they are like by the way they behave.

3 When one person describes another person, they are saying something about themselves as well.

4 Keep your characters moving, working, changing. Keep them under pressure.

5 Put your imaginary characters into situations that you know about, and show how they behave.

6 Put a version of yourself into situations that you don't know about, and show how you might behave.

7 If a fictional character is based on you, and you don't want readers to know this, change the details. Give them a different age, a different gender, different nationality, different job. But remember that some people will always assume that fictional characters are the author in disguise. The more you deny it, the more (as far as they are concerned) that proves it. Live with it.

8 You don't need to give a full head-to-toe physical description of a character unless they are unusual-looking and this is part of the story. Otherwise, stay focused on the small, telling details.

9 Avoid stereotypes. Make your characters live as individuals.

10 People are often contradictory. Let them be contradictory in your stories. Explore the contradiction, and let that be the story.

11

Dialogue

In this chapter, you will learn:
- *how dialogue can bring your characters to life... and life to your characters*
- *the difference between direct and indirect dialogue*
- *how to improve your skills as a writer of dialogue.*

Alice was beginning to get very tired of sitting by her sister on the bank, and of having nothing to do: once or twice she had peeped into the book her sister was reading, but it had no pictures or conversations in it. 'And what is the use of a book,' thought Alice, 'without pictures or conversations?'

(Opening lines of *Alice's Adventures in Wonderland* by Lewis Carroll)

Dialogue brings stories to life, and gives life to stories. Alice understood that, and so should we. Dialogue shows character and relationships. It moves events forward. It varies the pace of the story and the rhythm of the prose. It breaks up the page, giving relief to the eye from what, for Alice at least, seems to have been an off-putting mass of unbroken print.

Insight
Human beings are talking animals. So let your characters talk.

Direct and indirect speech

Imagine you are at a social event involving a sit-down meal. You want a piece of bread but can't reach the bread basket. What exact words would you use to get the person sitting next to you to pass it?

If the person is a stranger, you would probably say something blandly polite like 'Will you pass the bread, please?' But what if the person is a three-year-old child, or your boss, or someone with whom you are not on speaking terms, or someone who speaks only French? Any one of these circumstances would affect the way you phrase this ordinary request:

> ▶ 'Sweetheart, can you see that basket with pieces of bread in it? Do you think you could reach it and pass it to me very carefully so you don't spill any? That's a clever girl.'
> ▶ 'Sorry to bother you, Alan, but please could you pass the bread? Sorry. Thank you very much. Thank you. Sorry.'
> ▶ 'I know you're not talking to me, but would you pass the bread? If you're not planning to eat it all yourself, that is.'
> ▶ 'Er, madame… s'il vous plaît…'

These are all examples of **direct dialogue** – the use of the character's exact words. As an alternative, if you were describing the interchange in a story, you might avoid exact spoken words, and simply summarize:

She asked the person sitting next to her to pass the bread.

This is an example of **indirect dialogue.** Being a summary, it uses fewer words than direct dialogue. It takes up less space. And any approach to writing which does that is quite rightly of interest to the writer of short stories. But beware: the economy of expression that you achieve by using indirect dialogue may be a false one.

DISADVANTAGES OF USING INDIRECT DIALOGUE

▶ Indirect dialogue can be an efficient way of conveying information – the above example lets us know that someone at a meal table is asking for bread. But that is all it does, and it raises the question of why, if nothing else is going on, the author of the story would bother even to mention such a humdrum exchange.

▶ Indirect dialogue doesn't reveal what was said; it just offers someone else's interpretation of it. What the reader makes of this interpretation will depend on what they think of the person doing the interpreting. 'My teacher warned me that I would fail my exams if I carried on like this' tells us what the narrator understood the teacher to mean, but not what the teacher actually said, or how the teacher said it. If the author of the story wants the reader to take a view on the teacher's warning, then the teacher's words have to be shown. By seeing exactly what was said, the reader can form their own impression of whether the teacher's comments constituted a fair warning – 'Your test results show that your work is not yet up to the required standard' – or an attempt to humiliate: 'If you hand in that sort of rubbish, the examiners will laugh their heads off.'

▶ Indirect dialogue can be a bit lifeless. 'He told her he was having an affair' is a dull way of presenting what is probably a dramatic turning point in your story. What words did he use? Did he build up to it, or blurt it all out? In what context? How did he form his sentences? What details did he give? Was he penitent or defiant? Did he pause in his narrative? What for? Did the person he was talking to, say anything? Did the words of either of them display strong emotion? What emotion? How was it displayed? These are key questions in such an exchange, but the bald statement 'He told her he was having an affair' doesn't answer any of them.

Insight

Don't use indirect dialogue as a corner-cutting exercise. Give your characters real words to say.

Try this

Turn each of the following examples of indirect dialogue into direct dialogue, by writing the exact words that were spoken:

He confessed his sin to the priest.

The doctor gave us the bad news.

The midwife urged her to push.

He asked me to marry him.

ADVANTAGES OF USING DIRECT DIALOGUE

As a general rule, if what your characters are saying to each other is important enough to be included in the story, it is important enough to be presented in their exact words.

In Ali Smith's short story 'The Child' (in her collection *The First Person and Other Stories* (Hamish Hamilton)), the first-person narrator, a

Guardian-reading, Waitrose-shopping, bouquet-garni-buying woman, finds an unknown baby in the child seat of her supermarket trolley. She tries to get rid of the baby (referred to throughout as 'it') by handing it over to the appropriate authorities, but fails. So she puts the baby into her car and drives off with it. Predicament enough, you might think, but more is to come: suddenly the baby, who is plump and cuddly and sweet-faced and doesn't look old enough to speak, remarks: 'You're really a rubbish driver.' This is a prelude to a string of most un-*Guardian*-like sneers, wisecracks and one-liners on such subjects as women drivers, fat mothers-in-law, asylum seekers, and Iraqi prisoners with bags over their heads – all emanating from the sweet, pink, bow-shaped lips of the abandoned infant.

It's the direct dialogue that gives the story its power to shock. Babies aren't supposed to talk like that, but this one does. The same episode, presented in indirect dialogue or as summary – 'the child cracked a mother-in-law joke' – wouldn't have the same rawness. The child's exact words are part of the essence of the story.

Insight

It ain't what you say, it's the way that you say it.

WHAT ELSE CAN YOU SHOW THROUGH DIRECT DIALOGUE?

Relationships
Endearments, insults, formal and informal styles of address, private codes, can all be expressed in dialogue, as can tact, tenderness, condescension, respect and its opposite. Consider the difference between these two ways of approaching a delicate matter:

1 'Love, I'm sorry to mention this, but I couldn't help noticing – your breath isn't as sweet right now as it usually is. Would you like one of these mints?'
2 'Oi! Dragon breath!'

Origins
Where does the character come from, or sound as if they come from? Which country, which region, which social group? In our globalized and socially mobile age these things are more variable than they might once have been, and you don't want characters to sound like stereotypes, so use national, regional and class differences in

speech and vocabulary with a light touch. In Bernadette M. Smyth's prize-winning story 'Sightseeing in Louth'(in *The Fish Anthology 2010*; also available free on www.fishpublishing.com), a young Irish woman narrates the story of a visit to Dublin by her glamorous American male cousin. The characters' voices are distinctive and different, without ever being obtrusively so. With dialogue, as with so many of the skills of short story writing, less is more.

Insight

Be aware of the different ways in which language is used by different social groups. Without stereotyping, use these differences to give your characters distinctive voices.

One way of avoiding stereotypes is to start with yourself – after all, you are not a stereotype, are you? Try to identify the ways in which your style of speaking is a product of your background. Do you use vocabulary, quotations or sentence structures that you learned at school (what kind of school?) or from your parents? Do you use phrases from other languages or dialects? Why? Are there things you say at home that you wouldn't say in public (or vice versa) for fear of sounding rough, snobbish, work-obsessed, elitist, self-righteous or otherwise unacceptable? Are there things you go out of your way to say, to establish your position, get people on your side, make them laugh, or pull rank? Observe yourself, and observe others. Make notes. Use these notes when writing dialogue for your characters.

Age

Eight-year-olds don't talk in the same way as 18-year-olds, or 80-year-olds. Pay attention to how people's vocabularies and ways of speaking change as they grow older – whether it's contemporary teenage slang, or words and sentence structures that seem to come from a past era. Listen for examples. Use them.

Attitude to the person being spoken to

We all know people who interrupt, cut across the other person's speech, finish their sentences for them, or rudely contradict. Next time someone does this to you, examine the process: do they wait for you to pause, or just dive into the middle of your sentence, or even the middle of a word? Do they fabricate an excuse for turning the conversation back to themselves – 'Funny you should say that, it reminds me of a time when I...' or do they take it for granted that anything they have to say will be more interesting than anything you have to say? Do they appear not to have noticed that you were speaking at all? What is their interruption strategy? Capture it in your notebook, adapt it and use it in direct speech in your stories.

Attitude to themselves
More intriguing than people who won't let you finish a sentence are those who apparently can't be bothered to finish their own. They get halfway through, then say 'et cetera et cetera' or 'and so on and so forth' or even 'blah blah blah' or 'yadda yadda yadda'. They expect you to fill in the gaps. Or they keep demanding confirmation that you are paying attention: 'You hear what I'm saying?' 'You know what I mean?' 'You get me?'

State of mind
Is the character obsessed with something or someone? Do they keep returning to the same subject? Show this.

Being drunk
Some drunks become incoherent – you can show this in a few alcoholically distorted sentences. Some become maudlin or sentimental. Some get aggressive. Others may go the other way, trying to cover up their condition with over-the-top politeness and precision. All of these can be shown in dialogue.

> **Try this**
> Someone turns up an hour late and quite drunk for a date with their boyfriend or girlfriend. The partner demands an explanation. Write it as the latecomer would speak it.

Truthfulness or mendacity
What happens to spoken language when people are lying, or at least being economical with the truth? Some people become evasive; others give lots of unnecessary detail in the hope of bolstering their story. Show this in dialogue.

Whether they are trying to sell you something
Cold-callers are often trained to keep saying your name. (It's written in the script on the screen in front of them.) This is supposed to make the transaction more personal. It doesn't of course: it just signals loud and clear that it is a sales call.

DISADVANTAGES OF USING DIRECT DIALOGUE

With so much going for it, direct dialogue might seem to be the only
way of conveying speech in short stories. But it does have some pitfalls:

▶ If you stick too faithfully to the exact vocabulary, rhythms and
mannerisms of everyday speech, the result may be repetitive,
boring and difficult to read. Most of us don't speak in complete,
perfectly formed sentences: we backtrack, we stumble, we
hesitate, we use the wrong word, sometimes correcting ourselves,
sometimes not. On the page that sort of thing would be quite
difficult to follow, so you need to tidy it up, while at the same
time retaining the flavour of how the character speaks.

▶ If one of your characters peppers their speech with expressions
such as 'you know' or 'obviously' or 'at the end of the day', it's
fine to include that to establish their voice and character, but do
so sparingly.

▶ You have to know when to include dialogue and when to leave
it out. If someone is pouring someone else a cup of tea, you
don't normally need the accompanying chatter – 'Tea?' 'Yes
please' 'Milk and sugar?' 'Milk, two sugars, please' etc, *unless*
something else is going on. If the reader knows – and the tea-
drinker does not – that the tea-pourer is adding poison to the
cup, then the milk-and-sugar conversation takes on a special
poignancy, and is worth recounting in full.

▶ The reader needs to know who is speaking. Aim to make this
clear from what they say, and the way they say it. In cases where
this isn't possible, use 'he said' / 'she said' as necessary. This may

seem unduly repetitive, but it's better than forcing your reader to stop and go back to work out who is saying what, often losing the thread of the story in the process.

▶ Don't strain to find alternatives to 'said', unless this is relevant to the story. If someone who normally speaks loudly and clearly, suddenly starts muttering, that is worth mentioning. But if someone shouts unexpectedly, an exclamation mark will make this just as clear as 'he exploded'. Don't overuse adverbs to express how something was said: instead, use words that make this clear.

Insight

If someone says 'I'm going to chop off your fingers one by one, fry them and eat them', nothing is added by revealing that they said it 'menacingly'.

How can you learn more about writing dialogue?

PAY ATTENTION TO THE WAY PEOPLE TALK

Carry a notebook and write down what you hear. If it has no place in the story you are currently working on, save it for later.

This is not a charter for spying. I'm not going to suggest that you hack telephones or listen at keyholes, but if you are the sort of person who attracts unsolicited monologues from strangers, put them to good use.

It's not what I really want to do, minicabs. I want to be a London cabbie. A black cabbie. I'm doing the Knowledge. Trouble is, you see, London is like a woman. If you want to really know her, really get close to her, you have to give up everything else.

I had this girl in the back of my cab. Really nice-looking girl. Beautiful legs, I could see her legs. And I'm not being funny, but I could feel a sort of heat coming from her. She was sitting where you're sitting and I could feel the heat like she was well fed and well looked-after, you know what I'm saying?

And she told me where to go, and I said, 'Is that your mum's place?' Bit cheeky, but I said it. Because I thought she must still be living with her mum, to be well looked-after like that. But she said, 'No, it's my

> boyfriend's place.' I said, 'He must be some boyfriend, to look after you like that.' She said, 'He is. He cooks for me.'

If that person behind you on the bus insists on talking into her mobile at the top of her voice, why shouldn't you take an interest?

> That chap who said he would come round tomorrow afternoon. He sent me a text. He's not coming. Some cock-and-bull story.
>
> Something credulous about having an abscess on his nose or something ridiculous like that. I didn't believe it. I just think something better came up. I'd prefer it if he'd told me. He should have phoned me up. Sending a text isn't very professional, is it? It's what teenagers do.
>
> I'll phone him up and say, look, you come on this day or that day, or you don't come at all. I'll ring up the gas board and tell them what happened. I mean, I'd prefer to be told the truth. I can understand he's got a business to run and if a bigger job comes up he has to do that. I'm not, you know. But sending a text. Honestly.

PAY ATTENTION TO HOW OTHER WRITERS HANDLE DIALOGUE

Another way of learning how to write effective dialogue for short stories is to look at how other writers have done it.

In 'The Necklace' by Guy de Maupassant (it is often included in de Maupassant collections, and you can find several English translations online), a married couple in nineteenth-century Paris bicker about money. She is manipulative, he is insensitive; she wants him to buy her a smart new outfit, he wants her to stop moaning. All this is shown in the words they speak and the way they speak them.

In the title story of Bessie Head's collection *The Collector of Treasures* (Heinemann), a woman arrives at a prison in southern Africa where she is to begin a long sentence for murdering her husband. She is terrified, but, as her new companions start to talk to her, she relaxes a little. Through their talking, they show themselves to be kind, hospitable, courteous, and kindred spirits: they have murdered their husbands, too.

In 'The Things They Carried' by Tim O'Brien, a platoon of soldiers have just witnessed the shooting dead of one of their comrades by an enemy sniper. One of the survivors wants to deal with the shock and horror and grief by describing the incident over and over again. Another wants him to shut up about it. It's a dialogue about dialogue, about what it can and cannot do. It can't bring dead soldiers back to life. But it can invigorate your stories.

Sometimes, entire stories can be written in dialogue. Here is one written by me.

Meek & Mild

by Zoë Fairbairns

I don't want to go,' said the little girl.

'Yes you do,' said the father. 'You'll like it.'

'I won't.'

'At least give it a try,' the mother coaxed. 'You'll never know what you'll like and what you won't like if you don't try things.'

'I will,' said the little girl.

'Put your coat on,' said the mother.

'I don't want to wear my coat.'

'She'll have to wear it,' said the father. 'These places can be freezing.'

'Welcome,' said the vicar, 'to our special children's Easter service, and a very happy Easter to you all.'

'Happy Easter, vicar,' said some of the children.

'I didn't hear you,' said the vicar. 'I'm going to say it again. Hello, children, and a very happy Easter to you all.'

'Hello, vicar! Happy Easter!' the children called back, more loudly this time.

'Join in!' whispered the mother.

'I don't want to.'

'You've got to.'

'That's better,' said the vicar. 'And hello and happy Easter to all the mums and dads and carers.'

'Hello and happy Easter,' said the mums and dads and carers.

'It's warm in here, isn't it?' whispered the mother. 'Let's undo our coats.'

'I want to keep mine done up,' said the little girl.

'What do we mean,' said the vicar, 'when we say happy Easter?'

'It means Jesus rose from the dead,' said a little boy.

'That's right, he did,' said the vicar. 'So we're all very happy, and that's why we have this lovely display of flowers and Easter eggs round the altar, to celebrate the new life of Jesus and the new life in us all.'

'A non-sequitur if ever I heard one,' whispered the father.

'Sh,' said the mother.

'We'll all have a piece of Easter egg later,' said the vicar. 'But first I want to ask you one question. Do people still rise from the dead in the way Jesus did?'

'No, vicar.'

'That's right, they don't, not in the way Jesus did, but still when people die they live on in our thoughts and love, and we're here to celebrate that too.'

'Alleluia,' whispered the father.

'Sh,' said the mother.

'So where have you all been off to, looking so smart?' asked the neighbour.

'Well,' said the father.

'It's like this,' said the mother.

'We've been to church,' said the little girl.

'I didn't have you down as churchgoing types,' said the neighbour.

'Oh yes, we're regulars,' said the mother.

'I'm off to Homebase,' said the neighbour.

'I had chocolate,' said the little girl.

'No concern for their teeth,' said the mother through her own.

'Hello,' said the teacher. 'I'm Miss Peebles, and I'm going to be your class teacher.'

'Say "Hello, Miss Peebles",' said the mother.

'Hello, Miss Peebles.'

'I've seen you before, haven't I?' said Miss Peebles. 'At church. Some of the other children are playing in the Wendy house. You've probably seen them at church as well. Do you want to go and play with them, until it's time for prayers?'

'All right,' said the little girl. 'Bye bye, Mummy.'

'Bye bye, darling.'

'She seems to like it,' said the mother.

'Good,' said her friend. 'And you? What do you think of it?'

'They don't ram it down your throat,' said the mother. 'I think that vicar knows the score. I expect she had to go through a lot to get to be a vicar, so underneath it all she's probably one of us.'

'Good,' said her friend.

'Not sure about Miss Peebles, though.'

'Who's Miss Peebles?'

'Her class teacher. She looks a bit, you know, old school. But I suppose the vicar will keep her under control.'

'Good.'

'That's the third time you've said "good",' said the mother.

'Is it?'

'Which I take to mean you don't think it's good at all.'

'If I did think that,' said the friend, 'and if I wanted to say it, I would say it. I wouldn't need to be prompted.'

'What did you do today?' asked the mother.

'Nothing,' said the little girl.

'You must have done something.'

'Sums.'

'Good. What else?'

'Science.'

'What did you do in science?'

'Weighing things. And the vicar told us a story.'

'About weighing things?'

'About Jesus,' said the little girl.

'What about him?'

'He was kind,' said the little girl. 'He helped people.'

'That's right,' said the mother. 'There have been lots of kind men and women who've helped people, haven't there? We know some others, don't we? What other kind men and women do we know?'

'The postman.'

'Who else?'

'Florence Nightergale.'

'Florence Nightingale.'

'And Pocahontas. And Mary Poppins.'

'Mary Poppins is a bit different,' said the mother. 'She's not real, she's just a character in a story.'

'Is Jesus just a character in a story?'

'A lot of people think he's real.'

'Hurry up,' said the father. 'You don't want to be late for school.'

'I don't want to go to school,' said the little girl. 'I don't like it.'

'What don't you like about it?' asked the mother.

'I don't like the fire in the ground.'

'What fire in the ground?'

'There's a fire in the ground where you have to go if you're naughty.'

'No, darling,' said the mother. 'There isn't.'

'It's like if you burn your finger, but it's all over your body. And it hurts and you cry but the fire won't stop because you've been bad.'

'Who told you that?' asked the mother.

'It's in the window.'

'Don't you think they're a bit young,' said the mother, 'to be told things like that?'

'We certainly don't go out of our way to mention it to the under-tens,' said Miss Peebles.

'I didn't think people believed in that sort of thing anymore.'

'It's one of the more uncomfortable aspects of our faith, isn't it?' said Miss Peebles.

'Somebody's mentioned it to her,' said the mother.

'One of the other children, perhaps.'

'So who's been telling them?'

'We have no control', said Miss Peebles, 'over what they are taught at home.'

'She said something about a window.'

'Ah yes,' said Miss Peebles. 'There are some souls in hell at the base of our stained-glass window of Christ in His Glory. That solves the mystery.'

'I don't want her frightened like that,' said the mother.

'Is she frightened?' said the father. 'She hasn't mentioned it again.'

'She's probably forgotten all about it,' said the mother. 'Or else processed it. She was a bit like that with Peter Rabbit, when the baby rabbits got baked in a pie. First it was nightmares, then it was "read it again, Mummy."'

'And James James Morrison Morrison.'

'And the Dreadful Story of Harriet and the Matches.'

'And Matilda Told Such Dreadful Lies. It is a very good school,' said the father, 'apart from that.'

'Apart from that, yes,' said the mother.

10 THINGS TO TRY

1 Write down the three most hurtful things anyone has ever said to you. Then write the three most welcome things. So far as possible, use the exact words. If you find that you remember them easily, this suggests that the words were powerful. Use them in your stories.

2 Write five different ways of telling someone to go away – from the polite to the obscene.

3 Write a conversation between two people who, although on friendly terms, disagree over whether or not they should go to bed together.

4 Finish this sentence: 'As my grandmother/grandfather used to say...'

5 Write a conversation between yourself as you are now, and yourself when you were half your present age. Be aware of how the language differs.

6 Write the last conversation between two people who are ending their relationship (a business relationship, a friendship, a romance – whatever you like). Let their feelings show in the way they speak.

7 Write a story consisting only of dialogue between a politician and a heckler.

8 Write about someone whose way of assuaging loneliness is to spend hours ringing up call centres and engaging staff in conversation. Write some of the conversations.

9 Write a conversation between a person with dementia and their carer.

10 If you have a baby, a toddler or a pre-school child in your life, keep verbatim notes of the conversations you have with them. Use them in your stories.

12

You can't believe a word they say – the role of unreliable narrators

In this chapter, you will learn:
- *why a first-person narrator doesn't always get it right*
- *how to make creative use of their unreliability*
- *steps towards creating an unreliable narrator.*

In the previous chapter, we stressed the importance of conversations between characters in your short stories.

In this one, we look at a different kind of conversation: the one between the narrator of the story, and the person he or she is telling it to.

This is not necessarily the reader, or at least not directly. The 'Dear Reader' approach, beloved by some early English novelists, is rare today. The contemporary reader is just as likely to feel like an eavesdropper on a private conversation that the narrator of the story is having with someone else.

Fay Weldon's 'Delights of France, or Horrors of the Road' (in *Polaris and Other Stories* (Coronet)) begins with the narrator saying, 'Miss Jacobs, I don't believe in psychotherapy.' Miss Jacobs is, of course, a representative of that very profession. The reader's role is to listen in on their first session, wanting to ask the unavoidable question: *If you don't believe in it, why are you having it?*

The story provides some answers to this, as well as to the question of why the narrator has, for no obvious medical reason, recently become paralysed. These answers become apparent to the reader (and probably to Miss Jacobs), but they don't enlighten the narrator, who remains locked in denial, unaware of the story she is telling.

A comparable effect is achieved by Dorothy Parker in 'A Telephone Call' (in *The Collected Dorothy Parker* (Penguin)). The reader listens in while a woman waiting desperately for a call from her lover prays to God to bring this about. The more she assures God that she hasn't been pestering her lover, and the lover hasn't abandoned her, the more the reader comes to realize that both these things have in fact happened: it is the very neediness that is shown in the woman's prayers, denials and repeated phone calls that has exasperated her lover and driven him to dump her.

And in Duncan Bush's 'An Evening with Your Ex' (in *Tilting at Windmills: New Welsh Short Fiction* (Parthian Books)), the reader isn't so much eavesdropping as listening to what sounds like a bar-room anecdote: a recently divorced man recounts how he accepted an invitation to have dinner with his former wife, and, still nursing many grievances against her, set out to use the evening to wreak revenge. The laddish bravado with which he tells his story, and the cruelty of its ending, cast doubt not so much on the factual accuracy of what is being recounted, as the honesty of the emotions behind it. The clue is in the glib, blokeish title: that 'your' isn't second-person; it's a generalized 'your', as in, 'you know what it's like... an evening with your ex... they're all the same'. But they are not all the same: this narrator is hurting, whether he admits it or not, and he is going to see to it that she hurts, too.

What is an unreliable narrator?

An unreliable narrator is one who gives an account of events in whose literal truth the reader cannot quite believe.

This goes beyond the obvious point that all fiction is, by definition, untrue. Everyone knows it is untrue, so there is no intention to deceive. But when you use the unreliable narrator as a storytelling device, you are using the fact that, within the terms of the story, there *is* an intention to deceive.

Insight

When using a first-person narrator, always be aware of who the narrator is and why they are telling the story (a) in this particular way, and (b) at all.

The unreliable narrator may want to deceive someone else in the story, or the readers, or perhaps only himself/herself. Sooner or later, this deception becomes clear to the reader, though not necessarily to the narrator.

Skilfully handled, this approach will arouse a variety of emotions in the reader: curiosity, amusement, fear, pity, knowledgeable superiority, *schadenfreude* or concern for the narrator or another person in the story.

The alert reader of 'Delights of France, or Horrors of the Road' will spot that the narrator's husband – ostensibly so concerned for her that he has brought her to see the therapist, and is waiting in the waiting room to take her home after the appointment – is a major source of her illness.

Calling someone unreliable in this context is not necessarily a moral judgement. Narrators can be unreliable because they are sick or oppressed or in pain, or because they are too young, too vulnerable, too unaware or too far out of their depth to comprehend what is happening to them. They are under pressure, and so is their story. They may be drugged or bereaved or trying to be polite. They may be trying to make sense where there is no sense to be made. They may be awaiting surgery or execution.

Insight

The unreliable narrator reveals more than he means to reveal. Even his evasions speak volumes. He allows the reader the luxury of feeling one step ahead.

There is a sense in which all narrators are unreliable, including us. Just listen to yourself next time you are trying to explain yourself, or excuse yourself, or impress somebody, or talk your way out of trouble. The very fact that we are telling a story that involves ourselves invites the question of why we are telling it.

> **Try this**
> Remember an occasion when you were caught doing something you were not supposed to be doing: breaking the speed limit or your diet, playing solitaire on your computer when you should have been working, 'forgetting' to pay for something in a shop or restaurant. **Write down the exact words you used to talk yourself out of trouble.**

Do we give an unreliable version because we want to escape the consequences of our actions, are we after sympathy, laughs, forgiveness, or are we trying to get someone on our side? Do we just want to feel better about ourselves? Are we trying to impress someone so that they will go out with us or offer us a job, or are we just seeking to fill an awkward silence? Do we even know what we are saying?

Insight

When the narrator is unreliable, the very act of storytelling is a story in itself.

Alan Bennett, in his introduction to his collection of monologues *Talking Heads* (published by BBC Books), which have been successfully performed on stage, TV and radio, and which work just as well when read off the page, points out that 'to watch a monologue on the screen is closer to reading a short story than watching a play'. He describes his spectacularly unreliable narrators as 'artless. They don't quite know what they are saying, and are telling a story to the meaning of which they are not entirely privy.' In 'Bed among the Lentils', an English vicar's wife doesn't realize she is an alcoholic until her Asian grocer draws it to her attention while making love with her in the storeroom of his shop. In 'Her Big Chance', an unsuccessful actress convinces herself that she is on the brink of stardom – despite substantial evidence to the contrary.

Creating an unreliable narrator

Insight

Unreliable narration is all around us – statements and stories which are undermined by the way they are told.

The pop song 'I'm Not in Love', recorded by 10cc, is the lament of a man who insists he no longer loves his ex: the more he repeats this, the less true it seems. Unreliable narrators appear in jokes or one-liners ('I'm an atheist, thank God' 'The class system is dead, or so my butler tells me'), and in everyday anecdotes:

A woman friend of mine was telling me about her recent visit to a Turkish bath – a real one, in Turkey. She appeared to have been indignant to discover that all the masseurs were male, even in the women's baths. 'It's not what you expect, is it?' she said. 'Well, it's embarrassing. You're practically naked, and they were totally uninhibited in the way they touched you.' She paused, thoughtfully, reminiscently, before adding, 'It was the same when I went back the next day as well.'

Creating an unreliable narrator – other approaches

Write three lies about yourself – the more preposterous the better:

> - I have royal blood.
> - I can fix it for you to win the lottery.
> - I have a rare, incurable illness.

Choose your favourite, give it to a fictional character, and have them develop it into the opening paragraphs of a story. The paragraphs should be as convincing as possible: include evidence, examples, little confidences and asides, anything that makes the narrator sound sincere. Once you have reached a point where even you are starting to believe it, turn it on its head. Have the narrator say something which arouses the suspicion that there is more to this story than meets the eye. Or perhaps less.

> I have a rare, incurable illness. It's called Minimonian's Syndrome, after Dr Jaroslav Minimonian, professor of pneumomiasmic enterontology at the University of Sarajevo, who first identified it. He's a lovely man. So kind.
>
> 'I wish I could do more for you,' he said. 'I do really, but I have to put my own countrymen first.'
>
> 'Of course you do,' I said. 'Coming from a rich country like mine, I'd be ashamed to expect your health service to step in where my own is too blind, too blinkered and too penny-pinching to help me.'
>
> So far I'm symptom-free. Thank God. Because when it starts – no, I won't tell you. Why would you want to hear about what I don't even want to think about?
>
> And to think that the drugs that could cure me, exist now. Not in this country, but in Sarajevo. All I need is for someone to lend me £500.

Another approach is to get under the skin of someone who has done something they know they shouldn't have done. First, have them narrate what happened as straightforwardly as possible. Don't let them joke about it, or make excuses. Stick to the facts.

> I had nowhere to go for Christmas, so my friend Elaine invited me to spend it with her in her flat. On Christmas Eve, her boyfriend showed up. He flirted with me in front of Elaine, and I fancied him so I responded. Early on Christmas morning, he left her bed and came to mine. We stayed there for most of Christmas Day, enjoying each other, as well as the sounds and smells of Elaine cooking the turkey. Then we got up and ate it.

It's not a particularly edifying account, but at least it sounds reliable: nothing has been glossed over, excused or dressed up.

Now write it again, but this time show, in the way your narrator tells the tale, that she is starting to feel guilty about what she did. At the same time, she is denying her guilt and trying to convince herself that she behaved as a friend and Christmas guest should – or at least fell victim to circumstances beyond her control.

> It wasn't my fault that he came tapping at my bedroom door at three o'clock in the morning. 'Who's that?' I said. 'Father Christmas,' he said. And brought in a plate of mince pies left over from supper. Well, I couldn't turn him away, could I?
>
> I said, 'What do you want?' He said, 'Just somewhere to sleep. Elaine kicked me out, she says I snore.' I thought, yes, he is a bit of a snorer, I could hear it through the wall, but Elaine's a kind-hearted soul and she is going to be so embarrassed in the morning if she finds out he's spent the night on the floor. So I said, 'You'd better get in with me.'

Convinced? No, neither am I. But continue and complete this unreliable account. Or construct another one. If anyone asks, you can say it's not about you, it's about a friend.

10 THINGS TO KEEP IN MIND

1 Unreliability may be an annoying quality to encounter in everyday life, but as a storytelling strategy it can add energy, irony, insight and fun.

2 When using a first-person narrator, make sure you know who is telling the story, to whom they are telling it, and why.

3 If your unreliable narrator is addressing the reader directly, let them use intimate, conversational tones to draw the reader into the deception.

4 If the narrator is being overheard while talking to someone else, let their language be appropriate to the person they are talking to – or think they are talking to.

5 If the narrator's account is full of gaps, give the reader enough information to fill them in, or at least make an informed guess about what is missing.

6 Ask yourself what the narrator is hoping to achieve by telling this story in this way.

7 Ask yourself: what is the real story behind the one the narrator is telling? Is the narrator aware of it – fully, partially or at all?

8 Give the reader the opportunity to know more than the narrator – to be one step ahead.

9 Remember the last time someone told you a lie and you believed it. What words did they use to deceive you so effectively? Put them into the mouth of an unreliable narrator.

10 Plot your story not just around the characters, but around the reader's perception of the characters – perceptions which change as the reader comes to realize that he or she cannot entirely rely on the narrator's account.

13

<h1>Documentary stories</h1>

In this chapter, you will learn:
- *how Post-it notes can make your stories stick in your reader's mind*
- *how recipes and menus can stimulate your reader's appetite...*
- *...and other ways to use documents in your stories.*

Imagine you've got this appalling flatmate, someone foisted on you by your landlord. You want to live in peace, but some of this person's habits are more than you can tolerate. So you ask the flatmate to stop doing at least one of the things that annoy you – stubbing out cigarettes in the butter, perhaps. The flatmate agrees, but two days later is back to his or her old ways. So you ask again, more assertively this time. The response you get is angry and confrontational: the flatmate arraigns you with a list of the ways in which you, too, are supposedly difficult to live with.

It's our old friend the little black dress – a story involving people in a predicament, trying to move towards resolution. The resolution could be anything from murder, to eviction, to falling in love. But this time the little black dress is accessorized: write the story entirely in Post-it notes.

> Try this
> Go out and buy some Post-it notes. Choose two different colours, one for each flatmate. Write the first note – the one about the cigarette in the butter. Think yourself into the situation, and write what a person would write in such a situation. Note your use of language: is it sharp and brusque, coldly courteous, or does it make light of the situation with exclamation marks, apologies for bringing it up, and perhaps a smiley at the end ☺? Stick it on the imaginary door of the imaginary

fridge. (Or you could stick it on the real door of your real fridge, but if you've got a real flatmate whose manners are impeccable, it might be best to explain first what you are doing.)

Change to the other colour and write the response. Include the date, or at least the day of the week when the notes are written: this allows you to show time passing, or not, as the case may be. Write in a style that contrasts with the first note, showing the difference between the two flatmates and their attitudes to this dispute. No one likes being criticized, in a Post-it note or anywhere else, but this can be shown in different ways. For a few days, peace breaks out, and there are no more notes. Then (remember the date) there's another one – perhaps two, as the first flatmate, unable to contain their annoyance at the fag ash in the Lurpak, spills over into a second Post-it note – or perhaps uses one of a larger size, which the other flatmate will notice and comment on. And so the struggle continues.

Welcome to the world of the documentary short story.

What is a documentary short story?

It is a story which consists – partly, largely or entirely – of documents other than the story itself.

The most important characteristic of the documents (which don't have to be Post-it notes – they could be diaries, letters, transcripts, memos, emails, tweets, official reports, unofficial responses to official reports) is their lack of self-consciousness: there is no 'Dear Reader' here, no awareness of the reader. The documents in a documentary story have been created for a purpose other than telling the story that the reader is now reading. The authors of the documents don't know they're in a story.

Insight

With a documentary story, the reader is reading the documents over the shoulders of their authors and recipients.

A private diary, written to allow the diarist to let off steam and never intended for the eyes of anyone else, may arouse a variety of emotions – mirth, solidarity, incredulity, anger, guilt – in someone who is reading it without permission. Likewise a bundle of love letters that has fallen into hands other than the lovers'.

The documentary approach is one which has tended to be favoured more by novelists than short story writers. Examples range from Samuel Richardson's eighteenth-century epic *Clarissa*, in which a male sexual predator writes boastful letters to a friend recounting his carefully planned seduction of the eponymous heroine, to the more recent *Salmon Fishing in the Yemen* in which author Paul Torday uses contemporary media such as emails, office memos, television transcripts and Hansard parliamentary reports to tell a complex tale of international politics and extramarital love. But it is an approach that can also be effectively used to create short stories.

'Lunch' by William Boyd (in his collection *Fascination* (Penguin)) recounts a week in the life of a successful businessman. At least, he is successful at the beginning of the week, eating on Monday in the sort of restaurant where you pay £878 for lunch for seven people (*roulade de foie de veau farcie, millefeuille de fruits d'hiver*, service not included). By Sunday, after a week in which he has lost his job, his wife, his mistress, his child, and potentially a great deal of money, he is bingeing on crisps, sandwiches and a Mars bar with cheap wine in a buffet on a train. This tale of gastronomic decline and fall is told in seven lunch menus, and his notes on them.

In 'Chancery Lane' by Maeve Binchy (in her collection *Victoria Line, Central Line* (Coronet)), a 20-something dancer named Jilly Twilly meets a male barrister at a party, and later asks him to help her sue her ex-fiancé for breach of promise. Personally intrigued but professionally wary, the barrister contacts the friend who hosted the party, trying to find out more. Soon the barrister is more involved in the case than he ever intended to be. The story is told in letters.

In both cases the documents show not only what is happening, but why it is happening, why the authors of the documents are the sort of people to whom this sort of thing was bound to happen. If William Boyd's protagonist weren't so obsessed with his own appetites (as shown by his careful note-taking after every lunch), he might never have got into this mess. The tone of Jilly Twilly's letters shows that she is used to getting her way, and this occasion is no exception.

Sometimes the authors of this kind of story stop short of composing the story entirely of documents: instead, the documents are embedded in the wider narrative. In Fay Weldon's 'Christmas Lists', the lists are part of a more conventional narrative, and are sometimes discussed and quarrelled over by the characters. Sara Maitland's 'Gluttony' (in *The Seven Deadly Sins*, edited by Alison Fell (Serpent's Tail)) intersperses parallel tales of overindulgence and self-starvation, with recipes involving apples.

In storytelling, as in life, a document can be a mixed blessing. A story in a newspaper may be biased or downright false. But print lends authority. A letter sent by post can take several days to reach its destination, but is more private than an electronic one. An email may arrive within seconds of being sent, but it can only too easily be sent or forwarded (whether out of malice or carelessness) to someone who wasn't supposed to see it. A paper document can be torn up, burned or shredded, and so lost beyond recall; an incautious email may hang around and haunt its author for ever.

All of these possibilities may be as important to the story as the events they narrate. So when you write a document for a documentary story, always have these questions in mind:

▶ What is this document?
▶ What is the character trying to achieve by writing it?
▶ What conventions of language are generally followed in writing this kind of document? Will your author follow them or subvert them?
▶ What lies behind the writing of the documents in your story?

Let the story arise as much from the documents themselves as from the events they describe or cause. Why would two people living under the same roof choose to communicate through bits of paper stuck to the fridge? Is it shyness, fear of confrontation, or a wish to keep the dispute within limits? What happens to the notes in the long term?

(If the flatmates become lovers, the notes may be kept and treasured; if there's a murder, the notes may be tagged and bagged and taken away by scene-of-crime officers.)

Sometimes the boundary between the document and the story will become blurred. A quintessentially twenty-first-century mental health disorder has recently been identified: it's called Munchausen's Syndrome by Internet. Unlike plain old Munchausen's Syndrome, in which otherwise healthy people pretend to be ill in order to enjoy the sympathy and attention of medical staff, and Munchausen's by Proxy, in which they make someone else (typically their child) ill for the same purpose, Munchausen's by Internet involves pretending to have a particular illness and joining an online support group for sufferers. Some people do it for money, appealing for donations, but for others the online tender loving care of the group is all they want. It sounds pathetic, but no worse than that – until a member of the support group becomes overly emotionally involved and has a breakdown. One such pretence was uncovered when a support group member found a photograph on Facebook which proved that the so-called invalid was out partying at a time when she claimed to have been undergoing major surgery.

You couldn't make it up. But you could try.

Insight

In the early days of the Internet, many people saw its anonymity as an advantage: it seemed like fun, or even psychologically therapeutic, that users could pretend to be of a different age and gender, or invent a fictional life for themselves. These days we are more cautious, seeing how this kind of anonymity can be a cover for abuse. It's a development that opens huge areas of human wickedness, kindness and plain old oddity for the short story writer to explore, using postings, chat, error messages, blogs, adverts, games, tweets, pop-ups and emails – not forgetting those ever-more baroque legal disclaimers at the end of emails, which appear to invalidate everything that has gone before and are sometimes longer than the message itself.

All documents have their own language, starting with the salutation at the beginning of letters: 'Darling Cuddlebum' signals a different kind of letter from 'Dear Policyholder'. The ubiquitous 'Hi' at the beginning of emails signifies, to some people, a pleasing egalitarianism and informality; for others it is yet another symptom of standards breaking down as the world goes to hell in a handcart.

The same applies to abbreviations used in text messages, and the use of first names among strangers.

Insight

Document writers are almost always unreliable narrators, in the sense that they only tell part of the story — their own part, the part which has led them to write the document in the first place.

10 THINGS TO TRY

1 Write a global email from God to the human race, outlining changes that he has decided to make to one of the Ten Commandments to bring it into line with the modern world. Write one person's response, and the ensuing correspondence.

2 Write a story which consists exclusively of shopping lists.

3 A soldier going into action writes a letter to be delivered to her husband in the event of her death. She survives unscathed, but, following an administrative error, the letter is delivered anyway. Write the exchange that follows.

4 A woman secretly reading her husband's emails finds one which reveals that he has a six-year-old child by another woman. Pretending to be the husband, the woman writes to the child.

5 'Your server today was Kenny,' says the restaurant bill. On the back is a handwritten note: 'Hope you enjoyed your meal. K.' Touched by this friendliness, a customer writes back to Kenny. Write the letter, and Kenny's response. Continue the story.

6 Write three synopses of a short story. Each synopsis reveals something different about the author.

7 The borrower of a library book has written notes all over the margins. The library writes to the borrower, demanding money for the defaced book. The borrower writes back, denying that he has defaced the book and insisting that he has only improved it. He gives examples. Continue the story.

8 Write a list of every boyfriend/girlfriend you ever went out with. Now imagine the list falling into the hands of someone who would have expected to be included, but wasn't. They write to you. Continue the correspondence.

9 Write a story consisting entirely of medical appointments, and the patient's notes on them.

10 Years ago, someone sponsored a child in the developing world under a charity scheme. The child has now grown up, and got hold of her sponsor's home address. She writes to say that she will be flying in to her sponsor's home airport in two weeks' time. She is looking for somewhere to stay, along with her five children. Write the correspondence.

14

....

Fantasy and the supernatural

In this chapter, you will learn:
- *what magical realism is, and how you can use it in your short stories*
- *how to write horror stories to curdle your reader's blood*
- *how to write a creepy ghost story.*

All fiction is fantasy: as Helene Hanff noted, it is about things that didn't happen to people who never lived.

But the events *could* have happened. The people *could* have lived. In most of the stories mentioned in this book, everything that takes place is within the bounds of possibility.

Fantasy fiction, supernatural fiction, science fiction and magical realist fiction, on the other hand, take place in imaginary worlds where the rules of science, time and medical possibility, as generally understood in our world, do not apply.

The divisions between the categories are not clear-cut. Aliens with strange powers may come from outer space, from scientists' laboratories, from a magic spell or from somebody's subconscious; supernatural fiction includes ghost stories and horror stories; fantasy universes may contain witches, gods, vampires and/or humans with superhuman powers. It is sometimes difficult to identify the point at which one of these genres oozes into another.

Difficult and, for our purposes, unnecessary. In this chapter our concern is more with the practicalities of writing short stories set in worlds that cannot exist.

Therein lies the first problem. Short stories are short; worlds are huge, universes even bigger. By the time you have established them, your short story may be taking on the proportions of a novel.

As with other approaches to short story writing, it is best to keep things small and limited. Magical realism provides an effective context for this.

Magical realism

Magical realism is an artistic genre in which magical, fantastic or supernatural events take place in an otherwise realistic context.

Insight

The short story is a perfect medium for magical realism because, being short, it only requires the reader – and the writer – to suspend their disbelief for a short time.

Here's an example of a very short (210 words) magical realist story:

Butterfly Slippers by Rebecca Smith

I recall wondering at the time whether it was a mistake purchasing slippers with decorative butterflies attached. As it turned out my reservations were correct. I can never find them in the apartment, they constantly fly off, and are never together. I have now had to invest in a butterfly net, and must be careful not to leave the door or windows open. I have particular problems with the left one; it seems far more adventurous than the right. I arrive home to find it fluttering around the lounge, or hanging upside down from the ceiling. It wants to go anywhere but on my foot.

One fateful Tuesday I returned to find I had accidentally left a window open. After much searching I had to resign myself to the fact that the left slipper had gone. A month has passed, and I occasionally see it flying around the area. With winter approaching I have decided to buy another pair, this time with snails on; after all one slipper is of no use to anyone. They are not as pretty, but the advantage is they are much slower. In order to find them I just follow the sticky trail, invariably I locate them stuck to the wall near my potted plants.

This piece of flash fiction lures you in with its ordinariness. The pedantic choice of words in the first couple of lines ('recall', 'purchasing', 'my reservations were correct') suggests a narrator who is thoughtful, reflective, solitary. Nothing much happens in her everyday life. Then comes the flash: slippers are flying around the apartment, and she is chasing them with a butterfly net – as you would in a world where slippers come to life. There's no time for you as reader to think, *hey, wait a minute…* By the time you've done that, the story is over.

Insight

Magical realism is about finding the potential for magic in the everyday. It's a childish thing to do – but sometimes childishness is the appropriate perspective from which to write and read short stories.

Try this

Answer this question: *If you could be a supernatural being, what kind of supernatural being would you like to be?*

By a 'supernatural being', I mean any creature which either does not exist in reality as you understand it (examples might be mermaids, unicorns, tooth fairies, ghosts, Spiderman, Superman, werewolves, Zygons, avatars, angels, etc.), or else a real creature that has taken on unreal powers: it can be in two places at once, read minds, travel through time or come back from the dead. It can become invisible or do things that are inappropriate to its species – animals talk, humans fly. It might be an inanimate object (a statue, a toy, someone in a picture) that comes to life. The creature may originate in mythology or religion, in cartoons or computer games, in nursery rhymes, fairy tales, TV programmes, graphic novels, or in hallucinations, madness or imagination.

Choose the one you would most like to be, and think about it for a while. Research it. How have writers described such creatures? How have artists depicted them? In what times and cultures do they have their origins? How would it feel to be one of them in the contemporary world that you currently inhabit? What problems could you solve – or create?

Once you have a sense of who and what this creature is, what it could do, and how it could affect your reality, go back to Chapter 3, and refresh

your memory of the basic 'little black dress' short story structure.
Write a story using this structure, but when you get to 'something unexpected happens', let that something involve the supernatural.

For example: you might tell a story of a man who goes out shopping one afternoon and, although he has no particular interest in politics, gets caught up in a demonstration and trapped in a police kettle. He tries to talk his way out of it, or escape in other ways, but nothing works. Claustrophobia and panic set in. Our protagonist looks down at his body and realizes that he has turned into a dragon. He breathes his fiery breath on the police officers, who disappear in a puff of smoke. The demonstrators escape. Our protagonist — who may have returned to human form, or may still be a dragon, although no one seems to mind or even notice — continues with his shopping.

Other possibilities: someone who is trying unsuccessfully to learn how to swim, turns into a mermaid, and speeds up and down the training lanes of the municipal swimming pool at spectacular speed, flapping her tail.

A rejected lover, bent on revenge, realizes that he has the power to make his rival's house fall down, and does this.

Garden gnomes, statues, gargoyles or someone's secret collection of golliwogs or inflatable women come to life and become a benign or malign (your choice) force in the lives of your protagonists.

When writing a magical realist story, concentrate on keeping it dream-like, with vivid colours, strong sensory imagery and a weird kind of logic underlying the strangest events. Settings should seem odd, yet familiar. When magical events occur, they should seem normal. Don't comment on them. Don't express surprise. Don't explain. Remember the narrator in 'Butterfly Slippers'. She didn't waste time wondering why her slippers were flying about. She invested in a butterfly net and tried to catch them.

Other tales of the supernatural: fairy tales and fables

Fairy tales are what they sound like: stories which are peopled by fairies, elves, tree spirits, witches disguised as kind old ladies, or possibly vice versa. Animals are sources of wisdom, humans cast spells. Such stories are often of ancient origin, but they can be retold and reinterpreted by new generations, including you.

In 'The Ugly Sisters Strike Back' (in *Cinderella on the Ball: Fairytales for Feminists* (Attic Press)), Linda Kavanagh tells the story of Cinderella ('a frivolous, simpering creature who had been terribly spoilt because she was considered so pretty and dainty'), from the point of view of the stepsisters, both of whom are students (one of law, one of politics) and anti-monarchist in their politics. This influences their attitude to the prince.

In 'The Were wolf', 'The Company of Wolves' and 'Wolf-Alice' (all three are in her collection *The Bloody Chamber* (Vintage Classics)), Angela Carter uses the story of Little Red Riding Hood to write complex and haunting short stories about the sexual power and vulnerability of pubescent girls.

> Try this
> **What is your best-remembered fairy tale from your childhood?**
> What did it mean to you then, and what does it mean now? Retell it for contemporary times.

Fables are very short stories whose main purpose is to teach a lesson. Whether in their ancient form, as told by the Greek slave Aesop, or more recent creations, they tend to employ what would now be seen as the conventions of magical realism by having animals as characters, and having them behave in human-like ways. This simplifies the characterization and allows the reader to focus on – and believe in – the moral, which might be more difficult if the creature had human complexity.

In contemporary fables, the moral is adapted for modern times: in James Thurber's take on Little Red Riding Hood, 'The Little Girl and the Wolf' (in *The Thurber Carnival* (Penguin)), the little girl realizes at once that the wolf lurking in her grandmother's bed is not her grandmother, and she shoots the creature with an automatic which she happens to be carrying in her basket. Thurber's moral is: 'it is not so easy to fool little girls nowadays as it used to be.'

Try this
Refresh your memory of Aesop's fables, and those of the
seventeenth-century French fabulist La Fontaine. They are available
online. Choose one you like, and retell it in a modern setting. Give it a
moral of your own, preferably one which subverts the original.

The horror, the horror

Successful horror stories use cruelty, terror and the occult to evoke
fear and visceral revulsion. They invite you to look into your own
heart of darkness.

In Roald Dahl's 'Royal Jelly' (in *The Collected Short Stories of Roald
Dahl* (Penguin)), a human baby, fed on the eponymous substance to
correct a nutritional disorder, turns into a queen bee. In Daphne du
Maurier's 'The Birds' (in *The Birds and Other Stories* (Virago)), birds
declare war on humankind.

Horror stories make imaginative use of the paranormal, the occult,
phenomena that are biologically impossible but all too credible to the
imagination. They plug into the nightmare, the phobia, the irrational
fear and the rational one.

Try this
List your fears. Include your irrational phobias, as well as those
anxieties which may be only-too-well grounded.

- insect
- stranger
- cancer
- guillotine
- urban fox
- anaesthetic doesn't work
- going out without make-up
- having to live without sex

- insect crawling into my ear and
  eating my brain
- intruder
- stranger who turns up claiming
  to be my child
- life after death
- everyone knows what I did

Choose one and build a story around it. Be vivid and sensual in your
prose, and unflinching as you confront the fear. Carry it to its logical
limits. Then move on to illogical ones.

> What is the worst thing that can happen as a result of a woman going out without make-up? Embarrassment, self-consciousness, a belief that she is ugly? Or might the made-up mob, identifying her as an outsider, as 'not one of us', turn on her and tear her to pieces, using eyebrow tweezers, Botox injectors and shards of mirror?

Insight

When writing a horror story, ask yourself: 'What's the worst thing that can happen?' Then go one better – or worse.

In earlier chapters, we discussed structuring stories around a predicament, and the resolution of that predicament. With a horror story, let the predicament *be* the resolution – the only one the reader is going to get. One of the worst horrors is that there is no escape from the horror – so provide no escape. If your story is about someone who is scared of urban foxes, don't take the easy way out of letting them get into an encounter with an urban fox and come off best. Let the fox come off best. End on its foxy triumph, its dripping jaws.

Ghost stories

This category overlaps with horror, but is not the same: ghosts do not have to be horrifying. They can be benign, or just sad.

The eponymous 'Hanging Girl' in Ali Smith's short story (in her collection *Other Stories and Other Stories* (Granta)), a victim of judicial execution in a previous era, means no harm to Pauline, the contemporary woman she comes to haunt, and who tries to befriend her. Cissie, in Celia Fremlin's 'Don't Tell Cissie' (in *The Virago Book of Ghost Stories*), is an annoying schoolmate, who, excluded from the old girls' reunion because she always spoils everything, turns up anyway, but not before she has spoilt everything by being killed in an accident en route. Fay Weldon's short story 'Watching Me, Watching You' (in her collection *Watching Me, Watching You* (Coronet)) is told from the point of view of the ghost who lives in a house and watches generations pass through it.

Before you embark on a ghost story, decide on the ghost's role, which should be something more than running around in a white sheet and making strange sounds in the night. Let the dead interact with the living; let the ghost have an identifiable relationship with the person they were in life, and with the living people with whom they now interact. Get to the heart of what you think about the dead: do you believe they are gone for ever? If so, can they still be characters in your story? How? If they are not gone for ever, in what sense are they still around? In what form? Start there.

Try this
A hundred years from now, you will be dead. What will that feel like? Will you want to return? For what purpose? Write the story of yourself as a ghost. If you don't believe in ghosts, suspend your disbelief. A hundred years from now, medicine and technology will have moved on. Write about yourself as the first ghost that ever existed.

Any of the structures and plotting devices that we have looked at in this book can be used for ghost stories – you could have a person in a predicament that is resolved by a ghost, or the ghost could be the predicament. Stories which go in circles are particularly suitable for ghost stories – both have a haunting quality, as with the previously mentioned 'Don't Tell Cissie', at the end of which it becomes clear that Cissie is just as much of a nuisance in death as she was in life.

Science fiction and fantasy

Science fiction is concerned with events which, in the current state of humankind's development, are impossible. But if scientific advance continues at its present pace, they might occur at some time in the future.

Fantasy encompasses all the foregoing categories – magical realism, fairy tales, horror, ghost stories and science fiction – to create stories in settings which come from the writer's imagination, unimpeded by questions such as 'Could this happen?' Unrecognizable in realistic terms, they may nevertheless offer opportunities for play, symbolism and wisdom, albeit often in code.

The problem for the short story writer who tries to tackle science fiction and fantasy is that they are sometimes too big to handle in such a small, tight form. Fantasy in particular is without limits:

anything can happen. Where anything can happen, it's difficult for the writer to decide what will happen, and even more difficult to make the reader care.

Insight

When setting your story in an imaginary world, make sure there are realistic parameters that the reader can recognize and relate to. If it is a world whose creatures are invulnerable to what we recognize as danger, there is no point in sending your hero chasing after them with a gun.

Short stories which are realistic, or at least take place in recognizable settings, contain their own restrictions which will help to keep them short. But if you set your short story in a world of science fiction or fantasy, you have to know what that world is, what are its restrictions, risks and rewards. You can't set up a predicament, let alone resolve one, in a world where it is not clear what a predicament – that is, a situation of danger or difficulty – would be.

What's the point?

Some readers, writers and critics dismiss supernatural storytelling as little more than nursery tales, with perhaps an added veneer of sophistication to make them appear suitable for adults. They see this sort of writing as a childish evasion of the realities of life, which, examined with honesty, intelligence, curiosity and wit, should provide more than enough real-world material for any writer. Admirers of the genre, on the other hand, see it as a powerful challenge to restrictive and outdated literary conventions of realistic storytelling, as well as an effective code for speaking about what is otherwise taboo. If you want to write a story that would get you into trouble with the authorities (whoever they may be), telling it in code as a tale of the supernatural might give you the best of all worlds. David Lodge, in *The Art of Fiction*, notes how the Czech writer Milan Kundera used magical realism in *The Book of Laughter and Forgetting* to express ideas about the Czech communist party which, at the time of publication (1979), would have been taboo, and possibly dangerous.

You don't have to live under a totalitarian regime to have taboo thoughts, secret desires or a wild imagination. In Dom Nemer's short story 'Kew' (in *Tales of the Decongested*, vol. 1 (Apis)), a woman consumed with irritation for her fiancé, with whom she has not had an orgasm in six months, lures him to Kew Gardens, knowing that this will exacerbate his hay fever. She ends up being eaten by a Venus fly trap. In 'The Lilitree' by Mary Watson Seoighe (in *Dinaane: Short Stories by South African Women* (Telegram)), a contemporary South African couple deal with their servant problem by growing a housemaid in the garden, from a plant.

Try this

What are your taboo thoughts? What is your forbidden desire, or fantasy of revenge against an enemy? Give the desire or fantasy to a fictional character. And give them supernatural power to turn it into a kind of reality.

---

10 THINGS TO KEEP IN MIND

1 If your magical realist story leaves your reader feeling slightly dizzy, take that as a sign that you have got it right.

2 If your horror story makes your reader go 'yuk', the same applies.

3 To create a situation of horror, ask yourself 'What is the worst thing that could happen?' Then go one step further.

4 Ancient fables, fairy stories and legends have survived for a reason: they have something to say that people like to hear. Try to identify what that is, and build your story around it.

5 Flash fiction is an excellent medium for stories of the supernatural: by the time the reader starts to have doubts, the story is over.

6 Write horror stories from your own heart of darkness. What is your phobia? Claim it, examine it and use it.

7 If you want to write a fantasy short story, set limits on your fantasy world. Always be clear about what is and is not possible, what is and is not dangerous.

8 Write down your dreams. Use the stories and images that they contain, or to which they lead you.

9 If you want to write science fiction, and are not a scientist, check the scientific parameters of your story with someone who is. Your story should have authenticity and be credible in its own terms.

10 Use the story structures and plotting devices mentioned in this book to structure your tales of the supernatural. Or devise structures of your own. But don't imagine that, because your story is set in the world of the supernatural, it does not need to be structured. If anything, it needs it more – to save you and your reader from getting completely lost.

15

Research

In this chapter, you will learn:
- *why 'write what you know' is good advice*
- *why you know, or half-know, more than you think you do*
- *why, even if you know something, you may still need to research it*
- *how to find out about what you don't know.*

Traditional advice to new writers is that you should 'write what you know'. It is good advice, but you shouldn't let it limit you.

Your own world will provide material for a great many of your stories, but not all of them. So write what you know, but be ready to find out more about what you don't.

You may know more than you think you do. You may also know less: you may have lived in the same street for ten years, but could you describe it in detail? Probably not, unless you have been giving it the sort of attention that comes from deliberate, focused observation. You may know a lot about factory farming or fascinators or call centres in Mumbai or risk management, but is it the sort of information that would allow you to create characters, find predicaments and so energize a short story?

Insight

Research for fiction has three purposes. The first is to get your facts right. The second is to immerse yourself in the world that you are fictionalizing. The third is to point you towards new ideas and new directions for your story.

In the previous chapter, you were advised that before you started writing about a magical, supernatural being, you should do some research on it. The purpose of this was not so much to make sure you got it right – if the creature has been conjured up from the outer reaches of your imagination, who is to say that you have got it wrong? – as to immerse you in the world that you are trying to create. If you are writing a story about unicorns, spend some time in their world. There is – of course – a website called www.allaboutunicorns.com. Start there. Read the myths, look at the pictures. Listen to the music and find the films. Go to toy shops and look at the unicorn toys. If you feel foolish, try the 'It's not for me, it's for my niece' approach.

The same applies to more down-to-earth topics. For all I know there may be a website called www.allaboutgreengrocers.com which will be useful if you are writing a story about greengrocers. Better yet, find a greengrocer of your own and ask him or her to let you follow them around for a day. Occupy their world and make notes – not just on topics that you know you will need for your story, but on everything. Something you see or hear may change the story's direction. Let it.

Researching what you know

That heading may seem contradictory – if you already know something, why would you need to research it? But there are different kinds of knowing.

Researching for fiction is not the same as academic research, or journalism. You don't have to be objective, you don't have to cover everything or even know everything. You are telling a story, not presenting a report or defending a thesis. You are not looking for an overview, but for a small, telling detail. Suppose you are writing a story about a woman waiting for a man in a café. She shows her impatience and longing by eating all the sugar. It is more important that you let the reader know how the sugar is presented by the café (in bowls on the table that she dips into with a spoon, or in little sachets that she has to fetch from the counter and tear open?) than that you present the café's history or details of its decor.

If your story depends on factual content, make sure you get it right. If there is a real event, check the date. If you are in a real city, make sure all identifiable streets and buildings are in the right place. If you use Wikipedia, the online encyclopaedia, do so with caution. It is a conveniently accessible and wide-ranging resource, but anyone can contribute to it and anyone can edit its contents, so do not assume that what you read there has necessarily come from an expert. If accuracy matters to your story, check elsewhere, preferably in a book by an author of repute, published by a company that has something to lose by getting it wrong – as you have.

Insight

Nothing is more effective at undermining the intensity of a story than the irritation a reader feels when they realize that, on a point of important and easily verifiable fact, the author has got it wrong.

Factual accuracy is only one purpose of your research. Another is to stimulate your imagination, to light the spark that becomes your story. Short stories are about events, incidents – about small objects and small moments, moments of insight and intensity, moments of change. The sort of thing you don't know you are looking for, until you find it.

Find it by *not* looking for it, by looking for something else.

Try this

Make a list of every job you have ever done. Include holiday jobs and weekend jobs, part-time and casual work, and voluntary work. And don't forget that nightmare employment that only lasted one day and ended in fiasco.

Show the list to a friend and ask them to pick the job that looks most interesting. (Better to let them make the choice rather than do it yourself – their selection will be more unexpected than yours would have been.)

Write notes in your notebook about that job. Start with some of these questions:

- What was the official job title?
- Is that what you called it in private conversation? If not, what did you call it?
- Write a minute-by-minute description of the first five minutes of a working day.
- And the last five minutes.
- What did you wear?
- What was the best moment of the working day?

- And the worst?
- Was there any special language associated with the job – words, phrases, private codes, nicknames or jargon that an outsider would not have understood? Write some examples.
- Describe the place where you worked – the building, and your space within it.
- Who were you pleased to see?
- Who made your life a misery? How?
- What smells do you associate with the job? What tastes and sounds?
- What could go wrong? What happened when it did?
- In what circumstances did you leave?
- If they asked you to go back, what would you say?

The answer to any one of these questions might generate a story, but don't worry if it doesn't. Keep focusing on the questions. If you concentrate, and if you are lucky, you will spot, out of the corner of your eye, another little detail or incident or remembered object which sparks or evokes a story or image or fantasy: memories of the taste of those special Cornish pasties in the canteen may remind you of the day the health-and-safety people inspected the kitchen, and what they found; thoughts of your last five minutes in the job may evoke a tale of someone who decided to leave but, when it came to it, couldn't tear themselves away. So they organized themselves a leaving do that went on and on and on.

Insight

Many people take up writing as an escape from a day job that they don't like. If that applies to you, don't make the mistake of thinking that you shouldn't write about your job, or your former job. Of course you should. It's about time somebody did.

Researching what you half-know

Before embarking on research for a story, see how much you know already. Write down everything you can think of about the subject. Whether it is a lot or a little, the fact that it is already in your mind, without you having to look it up, suggests it has resonance for you.

Try this

Write down the year you were born. Subtract ten. You now have a year of which you cannot have any memories or first-hand knowledge, but about which you probably know, or half-know, quite a lot.

You will have heard your parents or other older people talking about that year; you will have some familiarity with its films, music, fashions and politics, as they will have been around in your childhood, or will at least have been discussed. Write the year as the heading of a page in your notebook, and **make notes of everything you know, or think you know, about that year,** even though you were not around at the time.

Let your thoughts flow freely: include guesses and things you only half-know but can check later.

1953. Coronation. The queen in a golden carriage. People camp out all night to see her. Someone (who?) climbs Mount Everest. Women wear stockings with seams up the back. My grandfather dies. Ethel and Julius Rosenberg in the US are executed by electric chair for spying – there's an account of it at the beginning of Sylvia Plath's The Bell Jar. *Plucked eyebrows. Roger Bannister (spelling?) runs a mile in four minutes. Children in school get free milk. Rock 'n' roll, or is that later?* Housewives' Choice *on the radio. Radio Luxemburg. The Ovaltineys. Song: 'Jesus wants me for a sunbeam'. Another song: 'You're a pink toothbrush, I'm a blue toothbrush'. Cold War. My parents first met at a party. He asked her out, she said no. (She was more interested in someone else.) Floods in East Anglia. Nuclear testing. Rationing ends.*

Make as many notes as you can. When you have exhausted your own inner archive, **write the year into your browser.** You will find thousands of entries – everything from international news reports to local weather, fashion notes, prices of everyday goods, and obituaries. Any one of these, even if it is not the main concern of your story, can add texture and conviction.

And talk to older people who remember that year. Ask if you can tape an interview with them about the year in question. Transcribe the tape verbatim, to get a feel for how they use language. Pay particular attention to their asides, their anecdotes, their personal impressions.

Now write a short story set ten years before you were born.

Researching what you don't know

It is unlikely that you will ever want to write a short story about a subject of which you know nothing at all. Something about it must have caught your attention.

Start there – with what you do know, or at least have wondered about. Write all that down in your notebook. Then follow the procedures outlined above – look at websites and books, visit museums and exhibitions. Look at objects that will feature in the lives of your characters. If you are allowed to touch them, do so.

If you don't know about something, talk to someone who does. People like being asked about their world. Well, some do. Some will tell you to mind your own business. In which case, ask someone else.

Most large organizations have press and PR departments whose sole function is to try and ensure that what gets printed about them shows them in a good light, or is at least accurate. Ask if you may come in and ask them some questions about what they do. They might even show you round their building, or let you shadow one of their employees.

Be curious. Do things that you wouldn't normally do. Is there a town, or an area of town that you never go to? Go there, and have a look around. Do you avoid football matches, cricket matches, concerts (pop or classical), or fashion shows? Go to one. Is there a public meeting going on in your neighbourhood of an organization you would never dream of joining, or indeed have never heard of? If it is open to the public, it is open to you, so be there. As you step into this alien (to you) environment, be aware that for most of the people around you, it is not alien at all; it is part of their normal lives. Keep your eyes wide open, your ears tuned, your fingers discreetly busy with your notebook, and find some short stories.

Insight

When researching the background to your stories, be ready to step outside your comfort zone. Don't bankrupt yourself, break the law or take silly risks, but if you can go where your characters go and do the things they do, you will write about them with more conviction.

Is there a particular newspaper that you never, ever read – because it is too downmarket, too upmarket, too left or too right? Read it, and gain some insight into the minds and preoccupations of people who read it every day.

When people come to your door trying to persuade you to vote for them or join their religion, do you turn them away? Why not listen to them for a change, and get a glimpse into their world? It might one day become a story.

Is there a clothes shop whose merchandise you admire but could never afford? Go in and try something on. Note your surroundings, note how you and other customers are treated, note the language that is used, note how these much-too-expensive-for-you garments feel against your skin. This will help to prepare you to write a short story about someone who shops there regularly.

> DISCLAIMER: Neither the author nor the publishers of this book can be held responsible for any unwise purchases you may make while undertaking this exercise.

Insight

Try to avoid using other people's fiction as research material for your own. Apart from laying yourself open to accusations of plagiarism, you will be using material that has already been processed at least once through the creativity of another fiction writer. If you process it again, it may emerge as appetizing as reheated tinned peas.

When should you do your research?

You could research the subject thoroughly before you begin your story. This ensures that you will be well informed from the start, and won't make mistakes which later have to be corrected. The trouble with this approach – researching before you write – is that you may not know what you are researching. If you don't know that your story is going to include a twenty-first-century child finding and playing with a Second World War gas mask, you won't know to go to a museum to find out what Second World War gas masks look like. There is also a risk that you may become so fascinated and well informed about gas masks that you will include material just because you have researched it – even though it doesn't really belong in the story.

You can avoid these difficulties by writing a rough draft of your story, leaving spaces for the material that needs to be researched. But this involves committing yourself to a version of the story which is not nearly as rich in detail as it would have been if you had all the material at your fingertips from the beginning.

The best approach is to combine the two approaches: start writing your story and keep going until you get stuck because you need to know something. Stop and research it. If while doing so you come across some new piece of information which could add a new dimension to the beginning of your story, go back to the beginning and rewrite, incorporating what you have learned.

10 THINGS TO KEEP IN MIND

1 Write what you know, but remember – you know both more and less than you think you do.

2 Immerse yourself in the world of your story. Find out much more about it than you will ever need to use in your story. That way, you will have plenty of source material to work with.

3 If your story depends on factual content, something your reader is likely to know about, get it right.

4 When researching the background of one story, be on the lookout for snippets of seemingly irrelevant information which might be useful in another story.

5 If you are using information from your own life, use questions to contain and organize it.

6 Be open to new experiences. Seek them out. Write about them.

7 If you don't know about something, ask someone who does.

8 Use your memory but don't rely on it: check.

9 If possible, do the things your characters do. Make their experience your own.

10 Let your writing tell you what you need to research, and let your research inspire your writing.

16

Do not skip this chapter

In this chapter, you will learn:
- *why grammar, punctuation, sentence structure and spelling matter*
- *how to get them right*.

Please don't skip this chapter. It is not very long, but it is important. It's about grammar, spelling, punctuation and the way you structure your sentences.

Some people were put off those subjects at school. As children, they never saw any point in taking sentences apart and putting them together again, or sorting words into categories. Nowadays many people suspect that these practices are irrelevant anyway: the informalities of the Internet have done away with strict rules. Language is a living thing, constantly changing, they argue; why should anyone in the twenty-first century (apart from pedants and intellectual snobs) care if infinitives are split, if modifiers dangle, or if the sign on the supermarket till says '9 items or less' instead of '9 items or fewer'?

The answer is that grammar is part of language, language is part of communication, and communication only works if there is common ground among the people who are trying to communicate. Of course, there is room for variation – that is how language develops. But grammatical rules are part of the common ground, or they should be. As a writer, you need to know what they are.

And as for the '9 items' sign in the supermarket – chances are that the person who wrote it wasn't doing so in pursuit of an ambition to write short stories and get them published. You, on the other hand, are trying to do that. So it's worth getting it right.

Another reason for wanting to skip this chapter might be that you think you know English already. You speak it, don't you? You don't need to know the rules, any more than you need to know the names of the muscles in your leg in order to be able to walk. On the few occasions when mistakes creep into your prose, they will be put right – often without you even noticing – by the spellchecker, the grammar checker and the style checker in your word-processing software.

You may be right. It is possible to express yourself clearly without consciously knowing or applying many of the rules of grammar; but it is equally possible to create misunderstandings from which only grammatical knowledge can extricate you. Consider the difference between the following:

> *A woman without her man is nothing.*

> *A woman. Without her, man is nothing.*

The words are the same; it is the punctuation which makes the difference.

Here is another example:

> *Showing off her new bikini, she was attacked by a shark.*

> *Showing off her new bikini, a shark attacked her.*

The first recounts a horrifying incident. The second sounds like a joke. Would you trust your software to pick up that difference – software that has been written by a stranger who cannot be expected to read your mind or know what effect you are trying to achieve with your story? How will you know that the software has followed the rules if you don't know what the rules are? It would be like expecting a calculator to work out your income tax without you, the taxpayer, having any knowledge of arithmetic or how the tax laws work.

Nor can you expect your spellchecker to pick up such common errors as the misuse of 'they're', 'their' and 'there'. Each of these words is correctly spelled: it's just that they mean different things:

▶ *They're* is an abbreviation of 'they are' – *They're in the kitchen.*
▶ *Their* means 'belonging to them' – *Peter and Joan are in their car.*
▶ *There* is an indication of place – *He's over there.*

Getting it right

This chapter isn't going to summarize every rule of good English: that would need a book in itself, and there are plenty out there. Some are recommended in the section called Taking it further at the end of this book. Or you could go back to school. The books that were used there to teach you grammar were probably well chosen. Get hold of copies and do some revision.

Equip yourself with a dictionary, either online or a book. Go for one with a well-established name and reputation, such as Oxford, Encarta, Collins, Chambers. Use it to check the spelling and meanings of words you don't know, and also to refresh your memory of words you think you do know but might have got wrong (or whose meanings might have changed). Depending on where in the world you are based, make sure the edition of the dictionary is relevant to the version of English that you use, and in which you want to write.

Insight

Don't just use your dictionary as a tool. Dip into it for pleasure. Find new words – or new meanings for old words. Don't go out of your way to use obscure, archaic or unknown foreign-sounding words just for the sake of it, but if you find one you particularly like, you could slip it into your story and so begin the process of introducing it into everyday language.

Find out whether the newspaper or magazine that you read publishes its own style guide. *The Guardian* does, as do *The Times* and *The Economist*. You won't always want your stories to sound like *The Guardian*, *The Times* or *The Economist*, but at the very least these guides remind you of what the conventions are (when do you use 'who' and when 'whom'?), what the issues are (when naming a foreign city for English-speaking readers, do you Anglicize it?), and the differences between words that sound similar (do you mean 'uninterested' or 'disinterested'?).

> **Insight**
>
> As a creative writer, you are allowed sometimes to break the rules to achieve a special effect. But first you need to know what the rules are and how they work – otherwise your reader may not be able to distinguish between a special effect and a mistake.

Numerous websites offer to teach you grammar and style: as with dictionaries, go for the ones that come from reliable sources, such as universities and reputable publishers. In the meantime, here are some general principles:

▶ Use the smallest number of words possible to tell your story to its intended audience. Or, as William Strunk Jr and E. B. White, the American authors of *The Elements of Style*, put it: 'Omit needless words.'

▶ Short, sharp sentences are preferable to strings of clauses linked by 'and' or (worse) commas. But see the next point.

▶ Never say never. If someone tells you 'never' to use adverbs or passive verbs, 'never' to split an infinitive or end a sentence with a preposition, or 'never' to write long strings of clauses, treat this advice with caution. It is one thing for a magazine or newspaper to have a house style on such matters; that is important for the consistency and appearance of the publication, and its brand identity. But you are not a brand, you are an individual writer trying to find and establish your voice. If someone else's style guide tells you 'never' to do this, that or the other, examine the reasons for the ban. If they make sense to you, then by all means keep your use of whatever has been forbidden to a minimum. But don't rule it out altogether. There are exceptions to everything, and your writing style is as personal to you as your facial features or your style of dressing.

▶ When you are writing direct dialogue, you can of course allow your characters to make grammatical mistakes and stylistic infelicities in the way they speak. In fact, you probably should, to make them sound fallible like the rest of us. (For more on this, see Chapter 11.)

▶ Use figurative language by all means, but make sure it does its job of creating a telling image in the reader's mind, rather than making things vague, abstract, non-committal or simply ridiculous. Don't mix metaphors. (For more on this, see Chapter 5.)

▶ Avoid jargon unless its use is a feature of one of your characters. If you use acronyms, abbreviations and initials, and they are key to the story, make sure your reader knows what they stand for.

▶ Many people whose day-to-day speech is clear and eloquent become complex, convoluted and pretentious on the page. Avoid this – trust your own voice. Don't strive to sound literary. Concentrate on being precise, and let 'literary' take care of itself. Keep asking yourself: what exactly do I mean? If you are having difficulty getting something down on the page, stop struggling and say it out loud. Then write what you said.

▶ When using a pronoun, always be clear which noun it refers to. This report during an outbreak of foot-and-mouth disease must have caused some consternation: 'On Monday, the first signs of the disease were identified in the sheep. On Tuesday, the Ministry vets arrived. On Wednesday they were all culled.'

▶ Be consistent. Tea pot, tea-pot or teapot? It doesn't matter. But make sure it is the same throughout the story – unless something in the plot requires that it be varied.

▶ Be sparing in your use of the exclamation mark! It is a nudge in the direction of being surprised, alarmed or amused by something; a dig in the ribs, a typographical 'geddit?' As such it can be intrusive, defensive and downright embarrassing, particularly when it is used to signify a joke but the joke isn't funny. Far better to let your words be surprising, alarming or amusing on their own.

Insight

Grammar, spelling and punctuation are not an optional extra in your stories: they are part of language, the medium with which you have chosen to work.

Provided you know what the rules are, you can of course, as a creative person, play with them and experiment. But get to know them first.

Besides reading books and websites on the subject, you can pick up the rules of English by osmosis: pay attention to the use of grammar in the short stories you read and admire. If a sentence seems particularly pleasing, look at its grammatical structure to see if you can identify how this helps to make it work. If you can't make head nor tail of what someone has just said, use your knowledge of grammar as a diagnostic tool to work out what went wrong.

10 THINGS TO KEEP IN MIND

1 Grammar is not an optional extra; it is part of language.

2 A good spellchecker is useful back-up, but it is not a substitute for knowing how to spell. The same applies to a punctuation checker and a style checker.

3 Be economical in your use of words, but not simplistic. If only a long word or complicated sentence will do the job, then use it. But if there is a shorter word which says the same thing, go for it.

4 Use style guides to widen your awareness of the choices you can make. But don't feel bound by the style requirements of a publication that might have priorities different from yours.

5 When characters are speaking, they don't have to speak in perfectly formed sentences. In fact, their dialogue will probably be more convincing if they don't.

6 Don't overuse exclamation marks.

7 If a publication you are hoping to write for has particular stylistic requirements, follow them. Otherwise, treat other people's rules as principles to be understood and considered carefully, but don't feel you always have to follow them, particularly when you have a better idea.

8 When reading, pay attention to the grammar and syntax of the writers you admire. Learn from them.

9 Enjoy words. Collect new ones. Read dictionaries and style guides for fun.

10 Develop the fascination which you, as a writer, must surely have for language. It is your tool. Keep it fresh, sharp and efficient.

17

Revisions, revisions

In this chapter, you will learn:
- *why real writers are rewriters*
- *ways to improve your work*.

When the writer Robert Graves left school, his headmaster's final words to him were: 'Goodbye Graves, and remember that your best friend is your waste-paper basket' (Robert Graves, *Goodbye to All That* (Penguin)). It was not, perhaps, the most encouraging remark for a teacher to make to an aspiring young writer, but the words contain a germ of truth.

Tearing up an early draft of a story and consigning it to the garbage – or despatching it to the recycling bin – is not a mark of failure. Neither are editing, tweaking, reviewing, revising and rethinking. They are signs that you are a writer, as opposed to someone who just jots stuff down and thinks that will do.

Anyone – well, nearly anyone – can jot stuff down. It takes a writer to polish and rewrite, to sharpen and to fine-tune, to cut and to check and to rearrange.

We've already looked at the importance of grammar, spelling, punctuation and sentence structure. This chapter looks at revising.

Insight

'If you feel entirely contented with your product, you have substantial grounds for alarm.' (Michael Baldwin)

But, you may be thinking, I have already laboured long and hard over my story. I've said what I meant to say. The story is as good as I can make it. Why do I have to change it?

You don't *have* to. You may be right: your story may indeed be as good as it can be. The pat on the back that you give yourself may be entirely justified. But you will only know that if you consider other ways that you could have written it. If, having done this, you come back to your original, convinced that you got it right the first time, that's fine. Your judgement is probably correct.

In the meantime, get another opinion. Present your story to your writing group, or show it to a writing buddy. Ask what they think, and pay attention to what they say. If they suggest ways in which your story might be improved, make a note of them and bear them in mind. But don't do anything yet.

Put your story away for a week or two. Forget it. Work on something else. Then come back and read the first story as if it were new to you.

What do you think? Did you enjoy it? If you had come upon it by chance in a magazine, written by a stranger, would it have caught your eye and held your attention? Why, or why not?

Insight

'I write every paragraph four times – once to get my meaning down, once to put in everything I left out, once to take out everything that seems unnecessary, and once to make the whole thing sound as if I only just thought of it.' (Margery Allingham)

Read your story aloud to yourself. Record yourself reading it, and play it back. Or ask someone else to read it aloud to you. That is a real test, and not for the faint-hearted. Hearing someone stumble over the prose that you thought flowed so freely can be a dispiriting experience. But it's an educational one, too. Make a note of the passages they have difficulty with, and see what you can do about them. Listen for inappropriate repetitions, unintended rhymes.

Listening to your story, ask yourself whether, if you had happened to switch the radio on and heard the opening lines, you would have stayed in the room to listen to the rest of it. Why, or why not?

Even if you can't see any specific, correctable faults in your story, you should consider alternative ways of writing it.

So where, you may be wondering, does all this end? How many revisions do I have to do? Am I never allowed to be satisfied with my work?

Many writers never are. If you attend an author's reading of a book and follow it in the published text, you will often find that the author isn't reading quite what is on the page: this is because they have just spotted a way it could be improved, and are kicking themselves for not having thought of it before the book went to press.

In that sense, revising and improving your work can indeed be a never-ending process. But on a practical day-to-day basis, it doesn't have to be; it can't be. You have deadlines to meet, even if they are only your own. Set a date by which your story must be finished. In the meantime, interrogate your story. Worry at it. Interrogate yourself. Answer these questions:

▶ Did you get useful feedback from the writing group or friend to whom you showed the story? What were the most helpful suggestions? How can you use them to improve your story?

▶ What about the *un*helpful suggestions? Be honest: were they entirely unhelpful, or did they annoy you because they contained truths that made you uncomfortable? How can you use those uncomfortable truths to improve your story?

▶ What do you think of the title you have chosen for your story? A title should give some information about the story, but should not try to summarize it, reveal the ending or hint at a moral. A key phrase from the story, or a recurrent one, is often a good choice. Even if you are completely happy with the title you have chosen, think of two alternatives. Then choose which of the three you like best.

▶ From whose point of view is the story told? Have you made a considered decision on this, and stuck with it? (If you need a reminder of the pros and cons of the different approaches, have another look at Chapter 4.)

▶ Are you happy with the characters' names? Consider alternatives.

▶ Which do you think is the liveliest, most engaging paragraph on the first page? Is it the first paragraph of the story? If not, why not? Move it up to the top of the page and rearrange the rest of the story to accommodate this change. Let your story begin where it really begins, not with a lot of verbal throat-clearing.

▶ When you were reading or listening to the story, did you get bored at any point? Did you find your attention wandering? Identify where this happened. Delete the boring bit.

▶ Have you followed the principle of showing rather than telling? If you need to refresh your memory of the difference between the two, have another look at Chapter 5.

▶ If a character in your story says something important, have you shown this by using direct dialogue, i.e. their actual words? If what they said was not important enough to be presented in this way, why did you include it in the story in the first place? Let your characters speak for themselves.

▶ Does the story give enough information on what the characters look like? Choose one character, and give him or her more physical presence. Does this improve the story?

▶ Can you find any mistakes or inconsistencies in spelling, grammar, punctuation, sentence structure or vocabulary? Correct them. See Chapter 16 for more on this.

You have probably come across the expression 'murder your darlings', which means that you should treat with suspicion – and probably delete – those passages in your work over which you laboured longest and hardest, the ones you are most proud of. You don't have to go that far, but do take a long, clear-eyed look at your final paragraph, or at least your final sentence. Delete it, and ask yourself whether the story is complete without it. In many cases, it will be. This is because the final paragraph or sentence is frequently not written for the reader at all. It is written to reassure the writer that he or she has covered everything. It belongs in your earlier draft, in the way that scaffolding belongs around a house that is currently under construction. Once the house has been built, the scaffolding is no longer required. If it is, the house needs rebuilding.

Consider this scenario. An editor has offered to publish your story – but only if you cut it by one-third, so that it will fit a particular slot. Would you do it? If so, how? Look again at your story and see which passages, in these circumstances, you might consider getting rid of, which of your darlings you might murder. If it turns out that you really can reduce the word-length of your story by one-third without doing it serious damage, that probably means it is too long. And if it is too long, you should cut it anyway, with or without the imagined pressure from the imagined editor.

Try this

Here is an early draft of the beginning of a story. It's pretty raw, and needs a lot of editing. Make a copy of it, and edit and revise it as if it were yours. Then look at the edited version, and see how it compares with your edited version.

My New Landlady
(raw version)

It was a raw autumnal day when I moved into Susan Ballantine's house. I felt sorry for Susan Ballantine. The whole point of having a home is that you can shut the door and exclude strangers, yet here she was, welcoming me into her home. During our exchange of emails, she had mentioned that she had recently split up with her husband, but beyond that I had no details about why she needed someone to share her house. She had put an ad on Craig's List and I answered it.

I wondered what misgivings she had as she showed me up to my room and left me there. She couldn't know how little trouble I was going to be: that she would hardly know I was there.

Most of the time, I wouldn't. At work I was signing up for all the overtime I could get. And I was on the lookout for a second job. I needed the money.

I wouldn't be importing smelly takeaways to eat in my room, or dirtying up Susan Ballantyne's kitchen with my cooking. I was planning to subsist mainly on raw food, the minimum necessary to sustain life. I wouldn't be throwing parties, smoking, keeping pets, having strange packages delivered or playing loud music. I had no sex life. (I lived in hope, though!)

I put my suitcase on the bed and looked around. Susan went downstairs and made herself a cup of tea. She considered bringing up a cup to her new tenant but decided no, start as you mean to go on.

Keep out of each other's way. Good fences make good neighbours, as the Bible says.

It was a small square room, not one that gave the impression of ever having been intended as someone's main residence: the bed, a largish single bed with drawers underneath, took up about a third of the space, and the only surface that you could sit at was a dressing table with a large, immovable mirror. I would have to watch myself eating. Not exactly comfortable. The wardrobe was small, the television on a shelf high on the wall, I would have to stand on a chair to switch it on.

The window gave a view of a small, neat pocket handkerchief of a garden, almost identical to the one next door and the ones in the next street, and the ones after that. The gardens and terraces faded away towards a pale horizon with a stripe of grey. Panoramic views of the estuary, you could say, if you were trying to sell the house.

There was a tap at the door. It was Susan Ballantyne. 'May I come in?' she said, asking for permission to enter a room in her own house. 'I forgot to give you the remote for your TV.' She was in her late 30s. She looked untidy and unkempt – blowsy, I might have called her, if I wanted to be catty. But why should I be catty about her? So what if she was several kilos overweight, had teeth full of fillings and looked as if she cut her own fringe? She had a nice smile, she was letting me move in with her, and from the sound of things she was all set to be the most liberal of landladies. 'Please don't worry that I'm going to make a habit of this, Ms Clarkson,' she stated, 'forever knocking at your door with rules and regulations. This is your home now, and you must come and go as you please, as I shall. But I just thought it might be helpful for both of us if we sorted out a few things.'

'Of course,' I said. 'And please call me Marie.'

She called me Marie, as we worked out a rota for using the bathroom and the kitchen and the washing machine.

'One more thing,' she said. 'Visitors.'

'I don't imagine I'll be having any,' I said.

'I'd be grateful if you didn't give them a key.'

'All right. If I do, I won't.'

After she had gone, I lay on my bed and cried and sobbed and wept. I was so unhappy. After about five minutes of this, she banged on the door and called out, 'Bit less noise in there, please.'

She's an unfeeling bitch, I thought in dismay. I've come to live with an unfeeling bitch.

My New Landlady
(edited version)

Consider alternative titles – Her Welcome? Raw Food?

~~It was a raw autumnal day when I moved into Susan Ballantine's house.~~ *Perhaps leave the weather for later. Get straight into the story, the relationship.*

I felt sorry for Susan Ballantine. The whole point of having a home is that you can shut the door and exclude strangers, yet here she was, welcoming me ~~into her home~~ in. *Don't repeat 'home'*

During our exchange of emails, she had mentioned that she had recently split up with her husband, but beyond that I had no details about why she needed someone to share her house. She had put an ad on ~~Craig's List~~ *craigslist* and I *had* answered it.

I wondered what misgivings she had as she showed me up to my room and left me there. She couldn't know how little trouble I was going to be: that she would hardly know I was there.

Most of the time, I wouldn't. *Wouldn't what? Say 'wouldn't be there' or 'wouldn't be'.* At work I was signing up for all the overtime I could get. And I was on the lookout for a second job. ~~I needed the money.~~ *No need to say this, it's obvious.*

I wouldn't be importing smelly takeaways to eat in my room, or dirtying up Susan Ballantyne's *Ballantyne or Ballantine? Be consistent* kitchen with my cooking. I was planning to subsist mainly on raw food, the minimum necessary to sustain life. I wouldn't be throwing parties, smoking, keeping pets, having strange packages delivered or playing loud music. I had no sex life. (I lived in hope, though!) *Delete the exclamation mark – it's coy.*

I put my suitcase on the bed and looked around. ~~Susan went downstairs and made herself a cup of tea.~~ *How would the narrator know Susan was making tea?* Susan went downstairs. I could hear her pottering about in the kitchen, filling the kettle, switching it on. ~~She considered bringing up a cup to her new tenant but decided no, start as you mean to go on. Keep out of each other's way. Good fences make good neighbours, as the Bible says~~ *A first-person narrator cannot report on the thoughts of another person. So either leave this bit out, or change it to something like this:* I imagined her debating with herself whether to bring me a cup of tea, and deciding not to. Start as you mean to go on, she would think.

168

Keep out of each other's way. Good fences make good neighbours, as the Bible says. *This quotation is not from the Bible, but from the poet Robert Frost. So either correct it, or use it to establish the narrator as a person who misattributes quotations, or who assumes that her new landlady does.*

It was a small square room, not one that gave the impression of ever having been intended as someone's main residence: the bed, a largish single bed *don't repeat 'bed'* with drawers underneath, took up about a third of the space, and the only surface that you could sit at was a dressing table with a large, immovable mirror. I would have to watch myself eating. ~~Not exactly comfortable.~~ *No need to say this, it's obvious.* ~~The wardrobe was small, the television on a shelf high on the wall, I would have to stand on a chair to switch it on.~~ *Use short, sharp sentences in preference to strings of linked clauses as here. Give some idea of what you mean by 'small', and avoid the unintended rhyme of 'small' with 'wall'. Substitute:* The wardrobe was too small for my things. The television was on a high shelf. I would have to stand on a chair to switch it on.

The window gave a view of a small, neat pocket handkerchief of a garden, almost identical to the one next door and the ones in the next street, and the ones after that. *Now is the time to mention the time of year and the weather, in the context of the garden – say something like 'Dahlias and geraniums shivered in the raw autumn wind.'* The gardens and terraces faded away towards a pale horizon with a stripe of grey. Panoramic views of the estuary, you could say, if you were trying to sell the house.

There was a tap at the door. It was Susan Ballantine. 'May I come in?' she said, asking for permission to enter a room in her own house. 'I forgot to give you the remote for your TV.' She was in her late 30s. She looked untidy and unkempt – blowsy, I might have called her, if I wanted to be catty. *Consider whether it is a bit late to introduce physical description, and whether this should have been said before. Perhaps it is OK: in their earlier exchange, the narrator was more concerned about the room than its owner. This is the first time she has really looked at her.* But why should I be catty about her? So what if she was several kilos overweight, ~~had teeth full of fillings~~ *how would the narrator know this?* and looked as if she cut her own fringe? She had a nice smile, she was letting me move in with her, and from the sound of things she was all set to be the most liberal of landladies. 'Please don't worry that I'm going to make a habit of this, Ms Clarkson,' she ~~stated~~ said, 'forever knocking at your door with rules and regulations. This is your home now, and you must come and go as you please, as I shall. But I just thought it might be helpful for both of us if we sorted out a few things.'

'Of course,' I said. 'And please call me Marie.'

She called me Marie, as we worked out a rota for using the bathroom and the kitchen and the washing machine.

'One more thing,' she said. 'Visitors.'

'I don't imagine I'll be having any,' I said.

'I'd be grateful if you didn't give them a key.'

'All right. If I do, I won't.'

After she had gone, I lay on my bed and cried. ~~and sobbed and wept. I was so unhappy.~~ *Don't overstate.* After about five minutes ~~of this,~~ she banged on the door and called out, 'Bit less noise in there, please.'

~~She's an unfeeling bitch, I thought in dismay. I've come to live with an unfeeling bitch.~~ *No need to say all this – it is already shown. Let Susan's words speak for themselves.*

Insight

The three greatest scientific discoveries of the twentieth century were: DNA, the contraceptive pill and cut-and-paste.

10 THINGS TO KEEP IN MIND

1 Don't expect to get your story right the first time.

2 If you have a friend or writing group whom you trust to give you a thoughtful opinion on your work, ask for it.

3 Listen carefully to other people's views on your story. Make a note of them. But don't act on them right away.

4 Put your first draft away and forget about it for a while before considering how it might be improved.

5 When you return to your story and read it afresh, ask yourself: if I encountered this story by chance, as the work of a stranger, would it hold my attention? Would I like it?

6 If you decide to rewrite, that does not mean you got it wrong the first time – only that you learned so much from writing your first draft, you are ready to attempt a second.

7 Use cut-and-paste to move your paragraphs around, particularly on the first page, where you can experiment with beginnings. Let the story begin where it really begins, not with a lot of verbal throat-clearing.

8 Be meticulous, but not compulsive. If you don't have an external deadline, set yourself one: whatever version you have on that date is your final version.

9 ...Otherwise you may go on rewriting forever, which is as bad as not rewriting at all.

10 Be ruthless with your final sentence. Does it need to be there? If not, cut.

18

Publishing your stories

In this chapter, you will learn:
- *how to identify the right publisher for your story*
- *how to approach a publisher in a professional way*
- *why you should enter competitions*
- *approaches to Internet publishing, to self-publishing and to radio and public readings.*

Publishing is a commercial enterprise. The publisher prints your story in a book or magazine, or posts it on a website, and hopes that people will pay money to read it. Alternatively, if the publication or website is free of charge, the publisher hopes that enough people will read your story, and the stories of your fellow contributors, to encourage advertisers to buy space alongside them. You get your story published and the publisher makes a profit, or at least covers costs. (You might even make some money yourself.)

This applies equally whether you are dealing with a small one-person publishing company operating out of someone's garage, or a multinational conglomerate. The multinational conglomerate may place more emphasis on the profit aspect (that's how it got to be a multinational conglomerate), but even the small press has to pay its bills.

This is not a reason for you to be cynically market-driven: the best publishers are the ones who combine a commitment to good-quality literature with skill at running a business. It *is* a reason to be professional about your work, and not to take rejection too personally.

What does 'being professional' mean?

It means finding out what publishers want, and offering it to them in the way that is most likely to elicit a positive response.

Start with the magazines you read. Do they publish short fiction – either regularly, or as part of a special feature? If so, do you have (or could you write) a story that would be at home on their pages? They probably have a website: go to it and click on where it says something like 'Information for contributors'. That means you.

Read what it says. Do they accept unsolicited contributions from freelance writers? ('Unsolicited' means they haven't commissioned it or even asked for it – you send it in speculatively, or 'on spec'.) Do they run competitions, or have certain times of the year when they invite outside contributions? Do they prefer paper copies or email attachments? What are their word-length limits?

If they don't offer any 'information for contributors', that could be because they are not looking for outside contributions at the moment. But if they have published short fiction recently, you could email them, or phone, saying something like this: 'I'm a regular reader and I notice that you published (NAME OF SHORT STORY) by (NAME OF AUTHOR) in your (DATE) edition. I have a story of my own which I would like to offer. Could you please give me the name and contact details of the person I should send it to?'

When you have obtained this information, follow up by asking, 'Do you have any special requirements as to how work should be presented?' The person you are talking to may not have the answer to this at their fingertips, but they may pass you on to someone who has.

Insight

If you find that none of the magazines you read publishes short fiction from outside contributors, it could be that you are reading the wrong magazines.

Approaching publishers

One way is to go into a branch of a large newsagent's and check out the contents pages of as many magazines as you can find which aren't sealed in thick, anti-browsing plastic and which you can get away with looking at before the staff start making pointed remarks about this not being a public library. Then go to the public library.

Have a look at the magazines they stock. Make a note of which ones publish fiction, and read the fiction they publish. Look, too, at the *Writers' & Artists' Yearbook* and *The Writer's Handbook*, which should be in the reference section. (If you can't find them, ask.) Published annually, both are full of useful information for the writer looking for markets for their work.

Go to www.theshortstory.org.uk and click where it says 'For writers'. At the time of writing this, 79 print magazines are listed as accepting short stories from outside contributors.

You can also find up-to-date information in the 'jobs and opportunities' section of the Writewords website, which is at www.writewords.org.uk. You can look at some parts of this site for free, but to access 'Jobs and opportunities' you have to subscribe.

OK, so you've discovered the name of a magazine that considers short stories by new writers... NOW WHAT DO YOU DO?

Get hold of a recent edition – in fact, several. Read them: particularly the fiction, but not just the fiction. Get a feel for the entire publication, for the editor's tastes and priorities. Don't even think about sending your work to a publication that you don't know well. Editors can spot from a mile off the sort of person who, while being graciously willing to write for their publication, has never actually taken the trouble to read it. Editors do not as a rule warm to such people.

If, having read several editions of the magazine, you feel that your story would be at home on its pages, send it off – in whatever format the publication requests.

THEN WHAT HAPPENS?

Probably nothing, for quite a time. Again, check the website: if it says something like 'we aim to respond to contributors within one month / three months', don't start reminding them before that time has elapsed.

Later, you could send in a brief, polite email asking them to confirm that they have received your story, and asking when you can hope for a response. (This is another advantage of making a preliminary phone call to find out the name of the person who deals with unsolicited manuscripts: not only does it improve the chances of your story landing on the right desk, it also means you know whom to chase.)

I would like to be able to say that the reason they are taking so long is that they are considering your story carefully and sending it to highly qualified outside readers. That might be true, but it might also be true that they receive so many unsolicited manuscripts and have so few staff that they haven't got to your story yet and may not get to it for many months. They may even have lost it.

Insight

NEVER send the only copy of your story to anyone. Always keep copies. If the story is on your computer, make back-ups. Keep the back-ups separate from your computer.

Waiting to hear from editors is a frustrating business for writers, not helped by the fact that there is no point in getting angry and standing on your rights, because at this stage you haven't got any.

What you have got are other stories. Keep sending them out, until you run out of places to send them to, or until you lose faith in the stories themselves. By the time that happens, you will probably have written more, so the fate of those earlier stories will no longer tug at your heartstrings as it might once have done.

WHAT HAPPENS IF THE PUBLISHER SAYS YES?

At the risk of sounding like Margaret Thatcher on the steps of 10 Downing Street after proclaiming a victory during the Falklands War – rejoice. For a newcomer to place a story in a magazine is a real achievement in these competitive times. Seeing your work in print will be a source of great joy to you, if not huge amounts of money. It will also look good on your writing CV: when sending out stories in future, always mention your previous publications.

WHAT ABOUT COPYRIGHT?

This is in such a state of flux at the moment – mainly because of new publishing technology, new laws and the Internet – that, even if I were a copyright lawyer (which I am not) giving a definitive statement of the law (which this most certainly is not), it would probably have been overtaken by events by the time you read it.

But the basic principle remains: if you write something, then the copyright in it (which means what it says: the right to make copies of it) remains yours, until such time as you sell that right, lease it, give it away or bequeath it. The magazine that wants to publish your story will probably ask for First British Serial Rights, which means you allow them to be the first British magazine or periodical to publish it. (If you have already published it elsewhere, tell them that.) All other rights should remain with you.

If, on the other hand, they say they want to acquire 'all rights' in the story – and if the magazine itself carries a notice to the effect that copyright in all the stories belongs to the magazine's publishers – be cautious. That, too, means what it says: if you agree to it, they will own the story as surely as if they had written it themselves. A lawyer once told me informally that this is so unfair that it would never stand up in court, but who wants to have to go to court to prove that they own a story that they have written?

Many new writers are so thrilled that anyone wants to publish their story that they will agree to anything. That might even be a good move, given that you need the exposure, and given that the chances of a single short story earning enough money for anyone to want to fight about it are so slight.

But it could happen. Short stories often adapt well into films ('Brokeback Mountain', 'Jindabyne', 'Far North', 'Company of Wolves' and 'The Loneliness of the Long Distance Runner' were based on short stories by Annie Proulx, Raymond Carver, Sara Maitland, Angela Carter and Alan Sillitoe respectively) and in those circumstances you would not want to lose control of your story or access to your share of the money. Hang on to your copyrights if you can. When you send out your work, always include a copyright notice on the title page, with your name and the date you wrote the story. (Once it is published, use the date of publication.) A copyright notice looks like this: © Your Name, 2011.

You can find more information about copyright in the *Writers' & Artists' Yearbook*.

Should I send my stories in for competitions?

Definitely. Even if you don't win a prize, you may be shortlisted, which is good for morale and good for your career as a writer, as it will get your name known. It may also lead to publication: some literary competitions publish a book containing the winners and shortlisted entries. If the competition that you are interested in is an annual event, it will probably have such books from previous years. Get hold of copies and read them before you send in your entry.

The Bridport Prize and the prizes awarded by Fish Publishing are among the best-known short story awards that are open to all. Find out more from www.bridportprize.org.uk and www.fishpublishing.com. The BBC National Short Story Award is open only to writers who are already published creative writers. You can find details – and a list of other short story competitions – at www.theshortstory.org.uk.

Always read the terms and conditions before you enter a competition. And if you do win a prize, or make it to the shortlist, don't forget to drop a short line to the judges saying thanks. The fact that they have chosen your story doesn't mean they want to be your best friend, but it's nice to be appreciated, and it will help fix your name in their minds for the next time your paths cross.

Insight

The first time I sold a short story to a magazine, I wasn't even offering it to them. I had entered it for a competition. A member of the magazine's editorial staff was on the judging panel; she wrote to me saying that, although my story had not won a prize, she had enjoyed it and would like to publish it in her magazine.

What about Internet publishing?

If you have your own website or blog, you can of course post your stories there. This is not, strictly speaking, publishing: no element of outside investment is involved, and no quality criteria are applied, other than your own. And you (let's be honest) may be biased. By all means showcase your work in this way – showcasing is a perfectly respectable thing to do when you are trying to get your work known and attract a following. But don't confuse it with the success that is signified by having your work invested in and published by someone else.

Here are just some of the many online short story publishing enterprises listed on www.theshortstory.org.uk:

- ▶ www.paragraphplanet.com specializes in 75-word, single-paragraph stories
- ▶ www.ladderwriters.com describes itself as 'an international creative writing website where by earning points you climb up the levels of the ladder to become a paid critic, contest judge and contest coach'
- ▶ www.slapastory.com invites you to submit a story right now 'to be reviewed by our editors'
- ▶ The Word Cloud, at www.community.writersworkshop.co.uk, is 'a free community where writers can read each other's work, offer comments and get feedback.'

You can find more information by looking in the 'Writers & Artists Online' section of the *Writers' & Artists' Yearbook*, and by writing 'online short story magazines', 'short story webzines' and 'short story ezines' into your search engine. And ask around. As I write this, I have just got back from a visit from my local bookshop where I was told about Shortfire Press, a digital-only publisher specializing in short stories from emerging and established writers – you can find it at www.shortfirepress.com.

The list of websites, webzines and ezines that publish work from outside contributors – sometimes for payment, sometimes not – is always changing. By the time you read this, some may have gone out of business, or transformed themselves into something else; new ones will have been created. If you find something that interests you but it asks you for money, exercise the same sort of caution as you would with any kind of Internet commerce. Make sure you know what you are paying for, and read the small print.

Self-publishing

Self-publishing used to be called, rather rudely, 'vanity publishing'. It was assumed that the only reason why an author would seek to publish their own work was because it wasn't good enough to attract a commercial publisher, and the author was too vain to admit this. Unscrupulous printers would prey on these individuals, extracting large sums of money to turn their manuscripts into inferior-quality books, which would then languish in heaps under the author's bed: effective distribution was never part of the deal.

It would be an exaggeration to say that the Internet has changed all that, but it has changed some of it by widening the range of options for self-publishers.

Insight

A book of short stories which has been published by its own author or authors is never going to attract the kind of respectful attention from critics, booksellers and potential purchasers as one which has a prestigious commercial publisher's imprint on its spine. But the prestigious publisher may not be interested. Fortunately this is no longer the only viable option.

With the right amounts of money, time, commitment and know-how, you – perhaps together with your writing group – can publish a collection of your stories, to your own quality standards. And you can distribute and sell them yourself, using the Internet, formal and informal networks, and shops, whether online or in the high street.

The *Writers' & Artists' Yearbook* has more information, as does a website called How to Publish Yourself in the UK, which is at www.publish-yourself.com. It starts by urging you to be realistic about why you want to self-publish, and what you hope to achieve: best-selling success is unlikely, but 'if you will be satisfied with seeing your book on the shelf in your local Waterstones and not be too worried that you blew a couple of grand to achieve that, then you should proceed.'

Depending on how much of the publishing process you are willing and able to take on, and how much you can afford to pay someone else to do, you will have to learn about book design, editing, marketing and selling, and may end up spending more time on these activities than you do on writing. But, says How to Publish Yourself in the UK, 'We have found the sales of the book are directly proportional to the time we spend on it. So the more time you put in, the more you get out.'

If you don't want to (or can't) do everything yourself and prefer to hire a self-publishing company, write 'self-publishing' into your search engine to find out who is out there. As with any other important and substantial business deal, do some market research before you commit yourself. Have a look at books particular firms have created, and decide whether their quality standards are good enough for you and your work. Contact the authors of the books and ask what they think of the service provided. Get on the phone to self-publishing companies, suggests Harry Bingham in the *Writers' & Artists' Yearbook Guide to Getting Published*, and ask what is the average number of copies of books they sell per year for each title they publish. It's a simple enough question: all they have to do is look at the total number of books they sell and divide it by the number of individual titles they publish. If they are evasive (and Bingham found that even the most outwardly respectable ones sometimes were), you should be suspicious.

If you decide to do it yourself, you will have to consider such matters as what other books are out there which might compete with your book, and how you can convince the book-buying public that yours is better. You will have to acquire permission to print any copyright material your book contains, decide what price to charge for your book, distribute it and sell it, finding different ways of saying, or signalling, 'Look, here's my book. How many copies would you like to buy?' You will even have to organize your own launch party.

So be aware of what you are taking on. But if you decide to go for it, good luck. Don't be put off by less enterprising people muttering about 'vanity publishing'. If in the middle of all that hard work you find time for the odd flash of vanity, you will probably have earned it.

Short stories on the radio

Radio is a good medium for short stories, but it is very specific in its demands: word-length, for example. If a story in a print medium or online is too long, it might just be possible to squeeze it into the space anyway. But a 15-minute slot is a 15-minute slot and you don't want the end of your story to be overridden by the pips. Check with the radio channel what length of story they are looking for.

BBC Radio 3 and Radio 4 broadcast stories, and sometimes publish them on their websites. Find out their current requirements by going to the BBC writers' room, which is at www.bbc.co.uk/writersroom.

Short Story Radio, at www.shortstoryradio.com, publishes and broadcasts short stories, and runs competitions.

> ## Insight
>
> When writing a story for the radio, bear in mind that your audience will probably not be giving it their undivided attention. Most radio listeners are doing something else at the same time: ironing, driving, gardening, cooking. They can be easily distracted, and if they miss what is going on in your story, they don't always have the option, as the reader of print does, of going back a few lines and reading it again. They've got to get it first time. So there is a premium on clarity and straightforwardness, on clearly delineated voices and consistent points of view.

Public readings

Liars' League is a public short story reading event which takes place in pubs. The organizers set a theme, and you send in your story in advance. The ones selected are read by actors. You can find out more at www.liarsleague.typepad.com.

And you can organize short story readings of your own, in your local bookshop, pub, community centre or coffee shop, or in your own front room. Is there a literary festival coming up in your area? Contact the organizers and ask if any events are scheduled at which new writers can present their short stories. If not, offer to organize one. Publishing means making something public. Use your imagination to find different ways of doing that.

10 THINGS TO KEEP IN MIND

1 The market for short stories is always changing. Keep up to date through the *Writers' & Artists' Yearbook*, *The Writer's Handbook* and writers' websites.

2 As a newcomer, you are unlikely to make serious money from publishing short stories. So do it for love, and treat the money as a bonus.

3 Don't even think about submitting a story to a magazine without reading several editions of the magazine first.

4 Many writing competitions publish anthologies of previous years' winners. Read them before sending in your entry.

5 Find out how the publisher or competition organizer wants work presented, and do it their way.

6 As far as content is concerned, if 'doing it their way' means violating your important values or principles, don't do it. Go elsewhere. Integrity isn't just a virtue: for a writer it is a resource. Compromising it is like poisoning your own well.

7 Posting your own fiction on your own website isn't publishing; it is showcasing or blogging. Showcasing and blogging are perfectly respectable things to do, as long as you don't confuse them with publishing. In publishing, somebody other than you is showing faith in your work: enough faith to invest time, money and expertise in bringing it to a wider public.

8 Kingsley Amis said: 'A bad review should spoil your breakfast but not your lunch.' The same applies to rejection slips.

9 If you are a student of creative writing, find out if your college or university publishes a literary magazine, and how to offer work to it.

10 Cultivate your personal contacts – but don't stalk them.

19

Why?

We are approaching the end of the book. You've spent a lot of time with it. You've read every page, you've done all the exercises, you've followed up on all the reading suggestions.

Or perhaps not. Perhaps you've only read the chapters whose titles interested you, and done the exercises that you thought would be particularly easy, or particularly challenging. That's fine. It's also fine if you turned to this chapter first, hoping it would throw some light on why you have this ambition to write short stories and get them published.

You know it is unlikely to make you rich or famous. Most writers of prose fiction who are rich and famous are novelists. Even if they write short stories as well, it is for their novels that they are best known.

Perhaps you really want to be a novelist. Good. Some of the contents of this book may help you, and you will find plenty more useful advice in *Write a Novel – And Get It Published* (Teach Yourself). But don't make the mistake of thinking that short stories are merely a training ground or rehearsal for writing novels. Is boiling a perfect four-minute egg a training ground for laying on a banquet? Does a 100-metre dash equip you to run a marathon? Is a one-night stand a good rehearsal for marriage? Of course not. There may be some overlap in the qualities they require, but some are appropriate for some occasions, and some for others.

So why write short stories?

Because you've got a story to tell, and it is short. That is the best reason. Something has happened in your life, or in the life of someone you know or have heard about or have imagined, and you want to set it down in words. You've considered the possibility that it might be a novel, but it hasn't got the substance or the sustainability of a novel. And you want it to be read quickly. You don't want the reader to browse through a few pages, then go off and do something else, then come back and read a bit more, which is the way many novels tend to be read. You want the reader to sit spellbound for five minutes or an hour or however long it takes to get to the end. Then, even though the story may only contain a small, brief incident, you want it to stay with them for a long time. You want the reader to wonder what happened next. At the same time, you want them to feel that they know.

Because someone has asked you to. It might be a personal request – a child saying 'Tell me a story'. Or it might be a professional one. Once you start publishing or performing your work, getting on to the shortlists of competitions, or becoming known in other ways, editors may approach you and ask you to write for them. Even if you are not yet at that stage, your eye might have been caught by a themed competition or a call for submissions on a website or in a magazine. Either way, your enthusiasm has been ignited: someone wants a story, and you want to write it.

Because you want to change the world. In the 1970s, I joined a women's writing group whose purpose was to write short stories that explored the ideas of the then-new women's liberation movement. We wrote stories exploring themes of sexual politics, and discussed them at regular meetings. We published two books (Zoe Fairbairns, Sara Maitland, Valerie Miner, Michèle Roberts and Michelene Wandor: *Tales I Tell My Mother* and *More Tales I Tell My Mother*, published by Journeyman, 1978 and 1987 respectively) and broadcast a BBC radio series *Tales We Tell* (BBC Radio 4, 1998). Did we change the world? Perhaps not all by ourselves, but there have been huge changes in relationships between the genders, and our group was a part – however small – of that. Is there an aspect of human society that you would like to see changed – preferably not through blood in the streets, but by piece-by-piece alterations of consciousness, brought about by single incidents or insights, triggered by small objects? Could you contribute to that change of consciousness by writing short stories? Do you have like-minded friends to work with, or could you find people, or do you prefer to embark on this project alone?

Because you love short stories, and you want to write stories that will be loved by other people. You've had that strange, spine-tingling experience of finding yourself in a story written by a stranger, and you want someone else to find themselves in yours.

Because you believe the short story is in decline, and you want to revive it. Good for you. Hubris is no bad thing in a writer. Go for it. Maybe when you die you will be buried in Short Story Writers' Corner in Westminster Abbey. Maybe there will be such a corner.

Because everyone is so busy these days that short stories are the only type of fiction they have time to read. Don't fall for that 'everyone is so busy' stuff. People will always find time for the things they really want to do. The problem is that a lot of them don't want to read fiction, or think they don't. Maybe you can change that. Maybe you can lure them into a fiction-reading habit with your short stories.

Because writing short stories is what you do. It's in your nature to tell short stories, just as it is in the nature of some other people to paint pictures or bake cakes or have lots of babies. Maybe you spend many hours on your day job – too many, in your opinion – but you know in your heart that your real vocation is to write. You don't feel happy or comfortable when you don't have a writing project on the go, and for you that means a short story.

Because you want to make pots of money. Forget it. You may make some, but you are unlikely to make enough from short stories alone, to pay your household bills – certainly not year-in, year-out. There are big-money prizes out there, and good for you if you win one. But you are not going to win big prizes every year. If serious wealth is what you are looking for, buy a lottery ticket.

But the best reason of all to write a short story is because you've got to. Bessie Head described the feeling:

Let Me Tell a Story Now...

I don't know why this is so but the first thing a person you've just been introduced to will ask you is: 'What work do you do?' I don't mean that he or she will ask it bluntly, just like that. They will hedge around a bit but eventually they will get down to the point and drag it out of you. As I say, I don't know why you dare to ask such a personal question but the reason that I do is because each person that I meet is a complete mystery to me. I have to find a quick and superficial way of piecing him together so that I know where I stand. I mean, I don't like to behave like a fool and some people instantly give you the feeling that you are behaving like a fool. I'm specifically referring to a hard-case lawyer I once knew. I struggled quite unsuccessfully to explain a delicate matter to him that needed just a bit of understanding and humane feeling and couldn't understand why he kept pulling me to shreds. Only later I learnt that the man's mind worked this way: 'Let us consider it on a judicial basis.' The poor man had completely identified himself with his work. He was all one-sided. A very dangerous type that because they can bust your ego to bits and you won't know what's happening to you, especially if your enemies are around and watching the terrific beating you are taking from one who knows all the answers.

In a broad sense then I would say that a person's character type makes him gravitate to a certain type of work. The fussy-fussy jumpy sort of woman becomes a typist where she can mess around all day minding other people's businesses. The rather heartless, dominating, you-actually-deserve-all-you-get type becomes a social worker. The tough guy with sadistic tendencies becomes a jail warder or a policeman. The dull, drab and toiling type a waitress, a shop girl or nurse. And so on.

I'm sorry but it has taken me quite a long time to get down to what I actually wanted to say. When anyone asked me this question, namely: 'What work do you do?' I used to answer 'Oh, I'm a writer'. Which is quite a lie, because I've hardly written a thing, and I've tried but I know I wouldn't be able to earn a living by writing. Working people are earning a living. I won't truthfully be a writer until I am *earning* something from the business.

When they said 'Oh, that's interesting, and what have you written?' I would say 'Well ... I have two unpublished manuscripts. One got lost in the post. The other got lost among the papers and rubble on a publisher's desk.' Nobody believed me of course and funnily enough I was telling the truth. I didn't have the guts to defend myself because I wouldn't have liked them to read what I had written. It was a hotchpotch of underdone ideas, and monotonous in the extreme. There was always a Coloured man here, an African man there and a white somewhere around the corner. Always the same old pattern. I tried to be poetic but even that didn't help. I just bored myself to death and I assumed that I would bore others too so I shut my mouth pretty quick about what I had written. If I had to write one day I would just like to say *people is people* and not damn White, damn Black and still make people *live*. Make them real. Make you love them not because of the colour of their skin but because they are important as human beings.

For instance, I would like to write the story about a man who is a packing hand at the railways and lives in one of the tumbling down, leaky houses in District Six. One year for his annual leave he decided to make use of the railway concession and take a free train ride with his wife to Durban. All the neighbours knew about it because they are a popular and sociable couple, as are most people in District Six. No-one has much of a private life in District Six. The neighbours make it their business to know all about you and they don't mind what your sins are. In fact, if it comes to the push they'll defend even if the law considers you in the wrong. The only suspicious man in District Six is the man who doesn't show his face and keeps a closed door. We are real good and jolly neighbours, minding each other's business the way neighbours should. We can't help it because we're all piled up on each other.

Well, to get back to the story. This man and his wife had a crowd of friends tagging along as they went to catch the train to Durban. Ticket and booking all arranged. Bags stacked with food for the journey. Things like roast fowl, fish cakes, meat balls and plenty of sandwiches and some booze. The wife, a huge, adventurous, generous, loud-talking, happy and carefree woman climbed on the train first. The husband remained on the platform with the friends. He was sort of glum with a I'm-figuring-this-thing-out look on his face. He always gets that look on his face when he's not too pleased about something. Just as the first warning bell rang he shouted with real terror in his voice: 'Ma, get off. Let's go home.' And that was that. He didn't even have to explain. Everyone understood. To leave Cape Town and go gallivanting around like some fool in a foreign place like Durban would be an act of the most vile treachery. Cape Town is his home. He was born here. He will die here. Besides, nobody in Durban would understand him. He has a very special kind of language. His very own. He has a special kind of face that is comfortingly reflected in the faces around him. Those faces swear with the exact same nuance that he does. They eat the exact same food. They have the exact same humour. Why go to that fool of a place called Durban? What is there in it for him? To leave Cape Town would be like dying. It would be the destruction of all that he is as a man. He just doesn't have the kind of pretentiousness that makes an American tourist come and gape at the Zulu dancers.

Well, there it is. I would like to write the story of the man and his wife who never took the train journey, but I can't. When I think of writing any single thing, I panic and go dead inside. Perhaps it's because I have my ear too keenly attuned to the political lumberjacks who are busy making capital on human lives. Perhaps I'm just having nightmares. Whatever my manifold disorders are, I hope to get them sorted out pretty soon, because *I've just got to tell a story*.

Have you 'just got to tell a story'?

The answer is almost certainly yes. After all, you've stayed with the book this far, haven't you? So do it, and good luck.

Taking it further

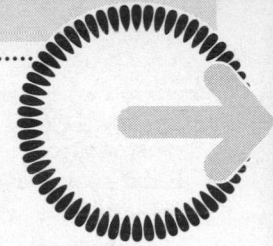

Here are some suggestions for further reading to help you explore the craft of short story writing and getting published.

Books about writing

Michael Baldwin, *The Way to Write Short Stories* (Elm Tree, 1986). This is unfortunately out of print, but second-hand copies are still available online (www.amazon.co.uk and www.abebooks.co.uk).

Julia Bell and Paul Magrs (eds), *The Creative Writing Coursebook: Forty Writers Share Advice and Exercises for Poetry and Prose* (Macmillan, 2001)

David Lodge, *The Art of Fiction* (Penguin, 1992).

Susan Sellers (ed.), *Taking Reality by Surprise: Writing for Pleasure and Publication* (Women's Press, 1994).

Books about getting published

Writers' & Artists' Yearbook (published annually by A & C Black).

The Writer's Handbook (published annually by Palgrave Macmillan).

Harry Bingham, *Writers' & Artists' Yearbook Guide to Getting Published* (A & C Black, 2010).

Mat Coward, *Success and How to Avoid It* (TTA Press, 2004).

For reference

Lynne Truss, *Eats, Shoots & Leaves: The Zero Tolerance Approach to Punctuation* (Profile Books, 2003).

Lesley J. Ward and Geraldine Woods, *English Grammar for Dummies* (John Wiley & Sons, 2007).

Magazines for writers

MsLexia – for women who write, PO Box 656, Newcastle upon Tyne NE99 1PZ (www.mslexia.co.uk)

Writers' Forum, PO Box 6337, Bournemouth BH1 9EH (www.writers-forum.com)

Websites for short story writers

www.theshortstory.org.uk

www.fishpublishing.com

www.writewords.org.uk

Index